PETROL LOG (HALIFAX)

INSTRUCTIONS FOR USE

1. The fuel state is to be recorded in the numbered columns hourly and whenever a tank is turned "ON" or "OFF."

2. A diagonal line is drawn when a tank is turned "ON."

3. A reverse diagonal line is added to form a cross when the tank is empty.

4. The calculated tank contents are recorded above the diagonal when each check is made.

CALCULATIONS.

TOTAL OXY TIME	6-50
TOTAL GEORGE TIME	NIL
TIME ON CIRCUIT	10 MINS
D/R ON LANDING	3CTHALF
FUEL LEFT	VES

Checked by ......

Tank No.	Tank Capacity	Tank Contents CONTENTS 7/0	1	2	3	4	5	6	7	8	9	10	11	12	13	14
Time		22.09	2309	2314	0009	0057	0104	0209	0143	0310	0400	0500	0530			
Port 1	247	247	172	167	247	247	233	161	125	125	125	64	64 14			
2	63	63	63	63	63	65	63	63	63	38		74	19			
3	188	188	113	108	140	140	140	140	140	140	140					
4	161	161	161	161	161	161	147	72	39	31						
5 & 6	245	245	245	245	131	25	25	25	25							
St'bd. 1	247	247	172	167	247	247	233	161	125	125	125	64	14			
2	63	63	63	63	63	63	63	63	63	38		74	89			
3	188	188	113	108	140	140	140	140	140	140						
4	161	161	141	161	161	147	147	70	39	39						
5 & 6	245	245	245	245	131	25	25	25	23			14				
Bomb Bay Front																
Centre	238	238														
Rear																
Overload—Port																
Fuselage—Port Overload																
Fuselage—St'bd.																
Total Fuel Left	FUEL LEFT 2046		1746	1726	1498	1286	1230	942	798	698	546	286	86			
	FUEL USED		300	320		760	816	1104	1248	1348	1500	1760	1960			
			1746	1706 1496	1496	1286	1210	948	798	698	546	286	86			
Gals./Hr.	G.P.H.		300	240	300	240	240	288	240	120	180	260	300			
Air Miles per Gal...	25 1/240R															
	Port Wing		OFF	ON	ON	OFF	OFF	OFF	OFF	OFF	OFF	OFF	OFF			
Position of Cross Feed Cocks	Fuselage		OFF	OFF	OFF	OFF	OFF	OFF	OFF	OFF	OFF	OFF	OFF			
	St'bd. Wing		OFF	ON	ON	OFF	OFF	OFF	OFF	OFF	OFF	OFF	OFF			

the
Nuremberg
massacre

the Nuremberg massacre

GEOFF TAYLOR

SIDGWICK & JACKSON

LONDON

First published in Great Britain in 1980
by Sidgwick and Jackson Limited

Copyright © Geoff Taylor 1980

ISBN 0 283 98646 8

Printed in Singapore by
Times Printers Sdn Bhd
for Sidgwick and Jackson Limited
1 Tavistock Chambers, Bloomsbury Way,
London WC1A 2SG

Front and back endpapers

The standard RAF flight engineer's log is reproduced here.
Despite the inevitable distractions encountered
in the bomber stream over enemy territory, the
loss of power on one engine of his Halifax EY-A
and a consequent emergency landing soon after
re-crossing the enemy coast, Sergeant D. G.
Davidson of No. 78 Squadron, Breighton, Yorkshire,
methodically maintained this log
throughout the Nuremberg raid.

For Mabel Rose Treglownow Taylor
1900-1978

Contents

Maps

Preface

The author does not set out to prove that the night of 30 March 1944 ended in catastrophic defeat for the RAF or in glorious victory for the Luftwaffe.

What he does attempt to achieve is, basically, to report on what it was like to be one of the many young men flying on this night of bitter confrontation between two of the most professional air forces the world had thus far seen.

Least of all does the author wish to throw doubt on the quality of leadership of the man who accepted the responsibility for the British strategic bombing offensive against Germany from February 1942 until the end of the war; the man who saw that the task was carried out, received less than his share of honours, and subsequently endured the criticism of those who were, as usual, wise after the event. That man was Marshal of the RAF, Sir Arthur Harris, GCB, OBE, AFC, better known to his war-time crews as 'Butch'.

Sources which the author consulted are gratefully acknowledged under 'Bibliography'.

He is also particularly indebted to Mrs M. E. Phillips, Air Historical Branch (5) RAF, Ministry of Defence, London; to Dr Arenz of the Military History Research Office, Freiburg-im-Breisgau, German Federal Republic; to Group Captain George Odgers and Squadron Leader Frank Doak of the Directorate of Public Relations, Royal Australian Air Force; and to Mr Harry Rayner.

Invaluable assistance was rendered by author-researcher Mr M. A. Garbett of Shirley, Solihull, Warwickshire, England, from whose prodigious files on the war-time history of the Avro Lancaster came many names, some narratives and a variety of photographs.

If, in this narrative, there appears to be a preponderance of dominion or British Commonwealth comment on the Nuremberg raid, it is only a reflection of the response to the questionnaires which the author sent out through the leading aviation magazines in the western world.

Distribution of 'de-briefing' questionnaires which formed the basis for much of the narrative in this book would have been impossible to achieve without the co-operation and kindness of numerous editors of newspapers and magazines in the United Kingdom, Canada, South Africa, New Zealand and Australia who readily published the author's request that survivors of the Nuremberg raid get in touch with him.

The author is especially grateful to those former pilots, navigators, flight engineers, bomb aimers, wireless operators and air gunners of Bomber Command who took the time and the trouble to answer his many questions about the events of this night that shook the RAF. In the narratives, ranks and decorations are given as they were on the night of 30 March 1944.

Units of measurement have not been metricated as, I feel, the imperial measurements system in use at that time will be more meaningful to the majority of readers.

Finally thanks to Audrey who, as secretary, typist, research collator, correspondent, coffee-maker and wife, flew every inch of the way on this one.

Geoff Taylor
Melbourne 1979

1   The Briefing

Few of the crews had any real presentiment of disaster. No more than usual, anyway. There was no implicit threat in the thin, early spring sunshine as it started the reluctant frost trickling from the camouflage-painted wings and the misted cockpit canopies and gun turrets.

The war, as always, seemed unreal and remote, offering no threat to the Lancasters, Halifaxes and Mosquitoes standing at rest on the circular, oil-stained concrete dispersals which, seen from the air, studded the green English airfields like clustered mushrooms.

For the crews whose names were listed on the typed battle orders distributed by the busy clerks of squadron orderly rooms, there was the usual speculation about the identity of the target for that night. However, there was still no special significance attached to the date on the battle orders now pinned to the notice-boards in the offices of the flights of all the squadrons.

The date was 30 March 1944.

It was a day which Bomber Command, Royal Air Force, was destined to remember.

When it began, the day was unremarkable. The briefing, after the morning's night-flying tests and a hasty lunch, had yielded no great surprises to alarm or awe or excite the listening crews.

So the target was Nuremberg. Since 1939 the bombers of the RAF had been to Nuremberg at least four times. Now they were going again.

As a target, Nuremberg had no particular ring of battle to

its name. To the crews of Bomber Command, Nuremberg, as such, meant little. It lacked the ferocious yet prestigious reputations of Essen, Bochum, Dortmund, Duisburg, Dusseldorf, Wuppertal, Neuss or any of the other blacksmith cities crouched by their arms forges in the misted, malevolent valley of the Ruhr—the infamous, legendary 'Happy Valley' of song and curse. Nor, as yet, did the name of Nuremberg have about it the awesome, ordeal-by-fire status of Berlin which was still, implacably, the 'Big City'. Nuremberg was no burned and blackened Hamburg, still angry enough and tough enough to be capable of exacting revenge for the firestorms which had raged through the great North Sea port during Bomber Command's fierce incendiary attacks in the summer of 1943, less than a year earlier.

The only really noteworthy thing about Nuremberg as the target for that night was its considerable distance from England, considerable when every mile was run under hazard all the way across German-occupied France and Belgium and over a Germany which the British and American bomber crews alike knew to be still savagely defended by the Luftwaffe.

For a Lancaster, a Halifax or a Mosquito, it was a long, hard trip across Germany to the point on the big briefing maps where Nuremberg's Kaiserschloss, a castle on a rocky outcrop to the north of the city, looked out over the fourteen bridges that elegantly spanned the Pegnitz river in a pleasant plain of Middle Franconia, a hundred miles north-west of Munich, itself a target of renown. Less picturesquely and more pragmatically, the waiting bomber crews knew only that Nuremberg and its river lay at Latitude 49° 26′ North, Longitude 11° 05′ East, about 470 miles east of another river, the Thames, where Greenwich Observatory marked the datum for all the world's longitude. The attack on Nuremberg would call for a deep penetration into Germany across a European sky whose sovereignty was still disputed by the radar, the searchlights, the flak and the fighters of the Luftwaffe.

With less than ninety days to pass before the dawn of D-Day and the Allied landings on the beaches of Normandy, the Luftwaffe was a mauled and wounded tiger—but it was still a tiger. Before the sun was to rise again the next day, bringing a pallid light to the bomber country of war-time England—the flat and misted counties bounded by the North Sea—the German tiger was to have drawn blood from the British lion in a night of savage and triumphant defence of Nuremberg.

As the dispirited sun sank lower over England and night stole like a dark intruder over the fens and furrows, canals and copses, pubs and steeples, there was no awareness of the imminence of catastrophe on the heedless, busy airfields of Bomber Command on that 30 March.

That afternoon and evening, though the grumbling, yawning bomber crews went phlegmatically about the routine of preparing for another night of battle, most of them would have admitted to the foreboding feeling customarily associated with seeing their names neatly listed for operations against a German target, particularly one as far east as Nuremberg. There was nothing unusual or shameful or significant in this attitude. It was a common enough reaction and for a very good reason: you could only play Bomber Command's version of Russian roulette so many times. Then, unless you were ideologically dedicated, Luftwaffe-style, or totally lacking in the capacity to draw logical conclusions from logical statistics, you began thinking about your chances not of living but of dying. The transition in attitude towards the logistically inevitable was slight but significant. The people who never worried about getting shot down were usually the inexperienced, the foolhardy, the careless and the clumsy. But they were shot down, as were the good and the true, the tried and the battle-wise, the very people whom you would have expected, by all the laws of probability, to have survived a tour of thirty or more operations.

Then, of course, there were the lucky ones. With an average loss rate of, say, five per cent on every major operation carried out by Bomber Command, the entire force would, theoretically, have been annihilated after every cycle of twenty operations. But there were those lucky ones who, it was always assumed, included yourself. Those and the endless procession of raw, young replacement crews, dumping their gear on dead men's beds. By mid-1944 a British or

American bomber squadron operating over Germany was no place in which to be playing at being Biggles.

If anything, the feeling of foreboding experienced between briefing and take-off was like the re-occurrence of a spasmodic tooth-ache. Suddenly, and sadly, you experienced it again; you put up with it; you hoped it would go away. Invariably it did, for the cure was take-off.

Most of the bomber crews on that quite unremarkable March day would also have suffered the usual, ambivalent psychological conflict between a deep-seated, atavistic desire to stay safely on the ground and a cerebral recognition of the cold, undeniable fact that if they flew on operations that night and came back then it was one less operation they had to fly before they finished their tour.

Most of Bomber Command's crews were to leave their briefings on Nuremberg that day thinking of it as just another long, cold, dark, dreary and probably unpleasant night's work. Their major concerns were not the defences alone, nor the target itself; it was the distance to and from Nuremberg— through some of the most heavily defended areas of German air-space.

Some of the airmen at the briefing, however, knew that Nuremberg was one of the sacred altars of Nazi Germany. Before the war, as schoolboys, they had watched newsreel films of Adolf Hitler, hoarse-voiced with hatred and almost incoherent with prideful emotion, reviewing his massed, goose-stepping, sieg-heiling legions at some vast, flood-lit, bannered stadium in this same German city. Then, many of them had marvelled secretly at Nuremberg's spectacles of brute power, so ominous yet so weirdly enthralling, so steeped in the neo-medieval mysticism of a new and aroused Germany once again on the march in Europe. Now, this night, they were going to Nuremberg . . . to drop bombs.

Some of the older British aircrew, bitter-mouthed from chain-smoking while they itched and yawned and belched and listened to the briefing, remembered days of pre-war travel and recalled that much of Germany's greatest beer was Bavarian, and Nuremberg was where they brewed a lot of it. Bombing a brewery, even a German brewery, seemed like sacrilege.

On their rostrums in the briefing rooms of the fifty-eight squadrons of Bomber Command committed to the night's attack, the intelligence officers were more definitive about the target. They knew of Nuremberg's cobbled streets, confined by buildings of medieval charm and distinction, which had rung to the thunderous sieg heils and the rhythmic, purposeful pounding of iron-heeled jackboots. The Bavarian city, they knew, was far more than a stein of good Bavarian beer or 50 000 strong German right arms raised in eager, obedient salute to a Fuehrer strutting Caesar-like between strange heraldic banners.

Strategically, the value as a target of this city of 430 000 people was that it ranked as one of the most important armament and engineering centres in southern Germany, with considerable capacity for the production of electrical equipment and electric motors—not to mention needles and pencils. An important junction in Germany's complex and efficient railway system, Nuremberg was also served by the Ludwig Canal which linked the Danube with the Main.

Such were the facts in the minds of the intelligence officers as, like frowning, earnest magicians, they uncovered the big wall maps with the blood-red route ribbons reaching irrevocably eastwards far across Germany to where Nuremberg's citizens were already, then, beginning to hurry home from work across the bridges of the Pegnitz.

Pausing for silence while the crews, like restive children kept waiting too long for the start of a birthday party, commented in their diverse but inevitably derisive ways on the choice of target for the night, the intelligence officers resumed their briefings.

The terms of reference for the crews, as summed up by their commanding officers, were uncomplicated: the object of the night's operations against Nuremberg was to ensure maximum damage to the target area.

If the directive from Bomber Command's underground headquarters near the peaceful Chiltern Hills west of London was soon to prove so empirical, the briefing, as usual, was detailed and entirely to the point.

Nuremberg was to be attacked by 795 aircraft: 462 Lancasters and 214 Halifaxes of Main Force, Bomber Command, led and supported by 110 Lancasters and 9 Mosquitoes of Pathfinder Force, Bomber Command.

The entire force of 795 aircraft from all Bomber Command groups—Numbers, 1, 3, 4, 5, 6 and 8 (Pathfinders)—would rendezvous in successive waves at Position *A*: 51° 50' North, 02° 30' East—approximately half-way between Great Yarmouth in Norfolk, and Bruges in Belgium.

From Position *A*, a navigational pinpoint in the sky above the lonely, disputed waters of the North Sea, the bomber stream would fly 130 miles south-east to Position *B*, 5 miles north-east of Charleroi, passing over the red-tiled roofs of Ghent and clearing Brussels by 10 miles to the south-east.

From Position *B* the bombers would then fly practically due east for a distance of 270 miles to Position *C*, 20 000 feet above a lonely valley in the forests of the Thuringerwald, 10 miles south-east of Meiningen, and half-way between Erfurt and Schweinfurt. (The latter town, ironically, only six months earlier on 14 October 1943, had been the target for an ill-fated attack by the heavy bombers of the USAAF, during which the unescorted Americans suffered disastrous losses.) On this long, straight, undeviating leg to Position *C*, which was the final turning-point for the run-in to the target, the bombers would fly 10 miles south of Liège, 20 miles south of Aachen, 25 miles south of Cologne, cross the Rhine 20 miles south-east of Bonn and skirt Wetzlar, Giessen, Fulda and Meiningen.

From Position *C* the bombers would swing to starboard on a south-easterly heading for 75 miles, leaving Schweinfurt 30 miles to starboard of their track and flying over Bamberg and Erlangen on the final stages of their run-up to the target area at Nuremberg.

After bombing Nuremberg, which was designated as Position *D*, the force would fly due south for nearly 30 miles to reach Position *E*, a navigational pinpoint above forested and mountainous terrain 7 miles south-east of Weissenburg. From there the bombers would, for the first time, turn onto a westerly, homeward course, flying for 80 miles on a south-westerly heading to Position *F*, 25 miles south of Stuttgart, a target with which many of the crews were already bitterly familiar.

The next course was a long leg which took the force for

300 miles, crossing the Rhine again 10 miles to the north of Strasbourg and passing between Metz and Nancy to approach Position *G*, 5 miles north of Epernay with Rheims 20 miles to starboard of track.

From Position *G*, 50 miles from a Paris under black-out, the bombers would head for Position *H*, over the coast of enemy-occupied France, between Dieppe and Le Treport. This 90-mile leg would take them out of enemy territory to run, for the second time, the gauntlet of the hostile, German-defended coast of northern Europe. The bombers would have Compiegne 10 miles to starboard, Beauvais 10 miles to port, Amiens 25 miles to starboard and, on the last 15-mile dash to the French coast, Abbeville with its crack, yellow-nosed Messerschmitt day-fighter wings, 25 miles to the north-east.

Over the French coast, with the crews reaching for coffee-flasks and cigarettes, the bombers would swing starboard onto another north-westerly heading which, after approximately 50 miles, would take them to Position *H*, in the thin, cold air over the English Channel, off the south coast of England. From there the homing bombers would cross the English coast near Selsey Bill and disperse individually to their own bases.

With its frequent changes of course to avoid heavily defended areas, and to keep Luftwaffe staff officers and controllers guessing until the last possible moment about the bomber stream's intentions for the night, the routing for the attack on Nuremberg was typical of Bomber Command operations at this stage of the air war. Planned in careful detail, the Nuremberg raid was by no means a hastily slapped together affair. Within a few hours, though, the critical factor in all the precise and calculated planning was to prove to be the long, straight, 270-mile leg east from Position *B*, over Belgium, to Position *C*, 75 miles north-west of Nuremberg.

As usual, to swamp the defences, the actual bombing attack by the 462 Lancasters and 214 Halifaxes of Main Force—a total of 676—would be concentrated. They would all bomb within seventeen minutes between 0105 and 0122 with zero hour set at 0010—a concentration rate of approximately forty bombers a minute or a bomb load going down every 1.5 seconds.

Since no aircraft in the bomber stream would be displaying navigation lights and many captains inevitably would be taking evasive action in the darkness of the approaches to the target, the risk of collision concerned some experienced crews as much as the threat of enemy defences.

The 110 Lancasters and 9 Mosquitoes of the Pathfinder Force which completed the night's total striking force of 795 aircraft had their usual intricately planned and precisely timed roles to play in the grand structure of the attack. As usual, the Pathfinder squadrons had two major tasks—to confuse the enemy with feints and deceptions on the way to the target and, once at the target, to mark it and to keep it marked for destruction by the 676 bombers of the Main Force. The questing Pathfinders were to begin their specialist work early that night on a special diversionary ploy designed to be the key of the operation. In fact, by an ironic turn of events, it became so—but for the benefit of the Luftwaffe, not the RAF.

As the first move in the night's tactics, the Pathfinders were to drop red route-markers—already familiar to the Luftwaffe as pyrotechnic sign-posts marking turning-points for the British bomber streams—near Aachen, twenty miles north of the bombers' actual eastward track across Germany to Nuremberg.

It was hoped that the watching and listening operations staffs of the waiting Luftwaffe would interpret the dropping of these flares as a turning-point in the route of the British bomber stream. Their suspicions should then have been confirmed by a feint attack from nine Pathfinder Mosquitoes on Cologne, further east again, between 2355 and 0007. Simultaneously, twenty Pathfinder Mosquitoes would be dropping target-illuminator flares, a radar-swamping cloud of metallic strips of 'window', and simulated Luftwaffe illuminating night-fighter flares further east again, over Kassel, a city still sensitive to the sound of air raid sirens since the fiery Bomber Command attack which had devastated it six months earlier on the night of 22 October 1943.

A line drawn from Aachen through Cologne and then finally Kassel could be interpreted as a logical track for an RAF attack on Magdeburg, Halle, Leipzig or the inevitable

Berlin. If the Luftwaffe swallowed this bait their night-fighter squadrons would be vectored to pursue and engage a phantom British bomber stream following a course which diverged north-east at a wide tangent to the track which the true force was actually flying.

Just thirty-one minutes after completion of the Pathfinders' 'spoof' attack on Kassel, two Pathfinder Mosquitoes would commence marking the real target at Nuremberg with green target-illuminator flares. Sixty seconds later, six other Pathfinder Mosquitoes would also bomb after having dropped 'window' at the rate of one bundle per minute, and then two bundles per minute, from within thirty miles of Nuremberg.

Six minutes after the first green target-illuminator flares were dropped, twenty-four more Pathfinder aircraft, high above a crouched and blacked-out Nuremberg, would drop blind marker illuminators at 0105. Two minutes later, at 0107, six more Pathfinders would drop visual markers. Two minutes later again, twenty-three Pathfinder blind backers-up would begin dropping from 0109 to 0122, while simultaneously twenty-two Pathfinder visual backers-up would be over the target with their target-indicator flares. At 0105, also, sixty-seven Pathfinder support aircraft would commence their subsidiary operations.

Depending on weather conditions encountered over the target, the Pathfinders would use either the 'Newhaven' visual ground target-marking technique or the 'Wanganui' sky-marking technique. The former would be used if the weather over Nuremberg was clear enough; the Main Force heavy bombers would then aim visually at illuminating flares and green target-indicator flares marking the target area. Salvoes of red and green target-indicator flares and then red target flares would indicate the aiming point.

If the Nuremberg weather was not clear enough for the Main Force heavies to carry out visual bomb-aiming on ground target-indicator flares, then the Pathfinders were to use the Wanganui method in which the heavies would aim blind at sky-marker flares parachuted by the Pathfinders to a pre-calculated position.

Intricately and meticulously planned as it was, the Pathfinders' contribution to the anticipated success of the attack on Nuremberg, and the Main Force heavy bombers' capability to exploit it, was still subject to a not entirely predictable factor—the weather.

On this occasion, though, the British meteorologists anticipated no difficulties. Forecasts for Bomber Command bases—always a matter of deep and subjective concern to crews returning from operations in the darkness before dawn—said that conditions would be 'mostly fit' all night with 'local smoke troubles' from industrial haze at bases of Numbers 4 and 6 groups in Yorkshire, with valley fog towards dawn, and slight showers on the east coast of England. Beyond the enemy coast, crews could expect to encounter broken residual convection cloud over Germany except in the south where cloud was expected to be layered. Over Nuremberg, large amounts of strato-cumulus would be encountered up to 8 000 feet with a risk of patchy medium cloud at 15 000–16 000 feet.

While there were many among the listening crews who were concerned about the possibility of cloud obscuring the target and the Pathfinders' flares, there were just as many who fervently hoped that cloud conditions that night would worsen, rather than improve, over Germany. The determined and deadly Luftwaffe night-fighter force included an increasing proportion of twin-engined fighters carrying their own airborne interception radar with which they could refine the vectors given them on R/T by ground radar controllers. For more than a year now they had forced Bomber Command to operate only on the nights when the moon was down.

Now, on this night of 30 March 1944, the British bomber force would be flying a long way in a straight line across Germany to a major target under the revealing light of a half moon. They would need all the cloud-cover they could get— and the crews, to a man, knew it.

Far away to the east, as the briefings ended on the airfields of Bomber Command and the time for take-off ticked closer on every watch, the moon was rising over Germany, bright and innocent and pitiless. This factor was forecast at the briefings, a calculated risk acceptable if there were the protective cloud-cover for the bombers. But, less obviously, great fronts of high pressure and low-pressure air were jostling each other like invisible giants over Europe and five miles above the blacked-out cities, towns and villages of Germany the high and lonely winds were stirring and shifting the cloud cover on which so much was gambled. This was a treachery, a meteorological malfeasance, which had not been anticipated at the briefings in England.

Once again, the cards for the nocturnal game of chance in the dark sky above Germany had been shuffled and dealt. The Luftwaffe was about to pick up a full hand of the highest cards in the pack. Unaware of this, the crews of Bomber Command climbed into their aircraft. Operations, as briefed had not been changed, delayed or scrubbed.

The target was still Nuremberg.

The night of 30 March 1944 had begun.

2   The Opposition

The backbone of the Third Reich's air defences in the west was still what the RAF's intelligence officers called the Kammhuber Line. Unlike its ground counterparts, such as the Siegfried Line on the Rhine, the West Wall on the Atlantic coast or France's abortive Maginot Line, the Kammhuber Line was not an orderly array of forts, dug-outs, pill-boxes, bunkers, tank traps, trenches, barbed wire, mine-fields, gun emplacements and machine-gun nests. Rather, it was simply a series of blocks of air space in which, by every known means, fair or foul, the Luftwaffe strove to destroy intruding enemy aircraft from the west, so denying, delaying or dispersing their attempts to penetrate the line and attack targets in the heartland of Germany proper.

The Luftwaffe by March 1944 had not been unsuccessful in its objectives. The crews of Bomber Command had come to know the Kammhuber Line as an area of night sky which they preferred to avoid by alternative routing, or to get through as quickly as possible.

Born on 19 August 1896, General Josef Kammhuber had entered a pioneer battalion of the German Army in August 1914, transferring to the infantry in September 1915. Remaining in the Reichswehr, he transferred to the air force in October 1933 and worked in the RLM (German Air Ministry) until July 1935; by February 1938 he was heading the Organization Staff at the RLM. During the German invasion of France, Kammhuber commanded KG 51, a long-range bomber unit; in July 1940 he assumed command of a Luft-waffe night-fighter division which by August of that year had become Fliegerkorps XII.

At that time, General Kammhuber had no knowledge of radar and his ground organization, largely drawn from the flak units, had no knowledge of the possible applications of radar to the air defences of Germany. In the autumn of 1940 a parabolic reflector ground radar, the Wuerzburg A, had been introduced but it was seized upon by the Flak Command as an aid to fire and searchlight prediction.

However, General Martini, the Luftwaffe's Director-General of Signals, had assigned to General Kammhuber six trained signals companies equipped with the Wuerzburg A radar. By October 1940, Kammhuber had set up three night-fighter zones in occupied Holland in the neighbourhood of the Zuider Zee and the estuary of the Rhine. Contained in an area of fifty-six miles long by nearly thirteen miles wide, the zones were directly in the path of RAF bombers flying to and from targets in the Ruhr. Each was occupied by a searchlight battalion and two Wuerzburg radars.

The immediate advantage of the inclusion of radar was that the night-fighter aircraft could be positioned singly in the zone by being linked through one Wuerzburg to a ground control. A master searchlight was linked to the other Wuerzburg and controlled a searchlight 'cone' for illumination of the British bombers. The whole area was equipped with a plotting control room, and three night fighters—one in each zone—could be vectored simultaneously. This system was known as *helle Nachtjagd* ('illuminated night-fighting'). Two other similar controlled searchlight areas were later established on the German coast near Kiel and Bremen.

Initially, German night fighters were successful against the British bombers passing through the *helle Nachtjagd* boxes of the coastal controlled searchlight belts, but Kammhuber completely appreciated the limitations that bad flying weather or cloud cover imposed on the illuminated night-fighting system. Even six-tenths cloud created considerable difficulties for the defenders.

Therefore General Kammhuber concentrated upon perfecting ground-controlled interception based entirely on the use of radar. His demands for additional radar aids eventually produced the *Wuerzburg Riese* (Giant Wuerzburg) with a radius of action of $37\frac{1}{2}$ miles.

The new ground-control interception procedure initiated by Kammhuber was similar to that of the first experimental controlled searchlight zones in that two radars were employed. In this case, however, the zone could be increased to a circular area with a radius of 37½ miles to correspond with the sweep of the Giant Wuerzburg. The course of a British bomber through the zone could be followed with one Wuerzburg while with the other the German fighter was followed and given vectors to intercept the target bomber.

The courses of both the British bomber and the German fighter were plotted on a table in a control room within the zone. Thus one fighter could operate within one zone, or box. So that it should not stray from the box while awaiting orders to intercept, the night fighter circled a radio beacon located within the area. The Luftwaffe code name for this system of interception was *Himmelbett*, literally 'four-poster bed'.

By late in 1940, the idea was put forward that a chain of these ground-controlled interception boxes placed close together, or even overlapping slightly, could form an effective barrier to the RAF's bombers and would also have the virtue of being operationally effective regardless of cloud conditions. Kammhuber therefore placed a line of air-fighting boxes in front of the Ruhr in such a position that any bomber force which took the direct route from England on a course to the Ruhr Valley was compelled to pass through the line of boxes, in each of which a night fighter was lurking, ready to pounce, while the Giant Wuerzburgs scanned the sky. This was the beginning of the famed Kammhuber Line.

Experience soon taught the RAF to avoid this area where night fighters were always patrolling, and they began flying into Germany north and south of the line.

Kammhuber replied by extending the line to cover the British detours. He had placed his line of boxes in front of the searchlight zones and encouraged his night-fighter pilots to attempt interceptions first under radar control and then, if that failed, to follow the bombers into the searchlight zones (which eventually were also equipped with radar). The original Kammhuber Line, which stretched no more than 150 miles in a north-east to south-west direction at the end of 1940, was first deepened by the addition of more boxes and then extended in length until, by March 1941, it reached from the tulip fields of Holland to Schleswig Holstein and Germany's frontier with Denmark.

The RAF still countered these moves with detours in their bombers' penetrations into Germany and raids increased in strength, being aimed not only at centres in the Ruhr but at other more distant targets such as Berlin.

By March 1942, Kammhuber had taken his line to the coastal areas of Holland and north-west Germany, including and re-equipping the original radar-controlled searchlight areas; there were also further extensions south-westwards towards Paris.

By July 1942, the line extended to the tip of Denmark and a further expansion of the spider web to southern Norway was in preparation. The Norwegian extension, however, could not yet be brought into full operation because expansion of the ground organization was outstripping the supply of aircraft and trained aircrews for the night-fighter force. By this time, the original night-fighting unit of the Luftwaffe, NJG1, had been expanded to a full *Geschwader* of three *Gruppen*, and three more *Geschwader*—NJG 2, 3 and 4—had been added.

The actual strength of the Luftwaffe's basic night-fighters now stood at 250 against an 'on-paper' establishment of 400. Of those 250, an average of 160 were serviceable.

Expansion of the Kammhuber Line continued throughout the remainder of 1942 and by the closing months of that year it had reached the south-east of Paris. Behind the line, in Germany, the radar net was also closing around the cities and towns that were the arms forges of the Third Reich, while in England the squadrons of Bomber Command were completing conversion from twin-engine Wellingtons to Halifaxes and Lancasters.

The entire system of the Kammhuber Line was now backed up by a network of early warning radar, and there had been erected large central plotting rooms, elaborately equipped and staffed, which gave a picture of the night's operations throughout the entire system. The stage was set for the massive nightly air battles soon to rage over Germany.

The four-engined bomber force which the Royal Air Force had built up was destined not to have things all its own way.

If the force were now to penetrate Germany without running the gauntlet of Kammhuber's formidable night-fighter defences it would be compelled to make time and fuel-wasting detours either to the south of Paris or to the north of Denmark. RAF raids which were routed through the line could only expect to meet dangerous and determined opposition. The nostalgic concept of airmen adversaries being chivalrous knights of the air had gone forever; from now, flying on operations with Bomber Command was finally to become as romantic a military occupation as had been the lot of the infantry in the trenches of 1914–18.

Up to this time, the logistic conception of a bomber stream led to the target by a specialist force of pathfinder crews was still unknown. The raiding British forces, with aircraft flying independently, still sought to steal through the line like burglars in the night while one Luftwaffe box after another vectored its waiting, orbiting night fighter to the attack with accurate and usually deadly effect.

In the middle of 1943, however, the workings of the Kammhuber Line had been compromised, with Bomber Command concentrating its bombers in a tightly timed stream which swamped the few boxes through which it swarmed. Overnight, the Luftwaffe system of vectoring its fighters onto their targets had been set a new and formidable problem.

As was to happen so often in the unceasing, nightly struggle between the two air forces, the boffins, the back-room boys, the scientists and the technologists in their laboratories were as much involved in the conflict as the aircrew and the ground staff of both military air arms. By July 1943 the whole system of German air defence had been taken by surprise with the electronic jamming of the radar with 'window', metallic strips of carefully calculated size which were showered down by the advancing British bomber force.

Untold industrial, scientific and military effort had been invested in General Kammhuber's line. Suddenly it had become an expensive and useless luxury and it was now necessary to reorganize the whole system of German night-fighter air defence.

With characteristic energy and efficiency, the Germans

16

reacted to the threat, and so far as Bomber Command crews were concerned by 30 March 1944, the Luftwaffe was well and truly back in the game.

During the first three months of 1944, the night fighters of the Luftwaffe had struck back hard. In twelve weeks, 763 four-engined RAF bombers and their crews had been shot down in major night raids against German cities. The loss was equivalent to eighty per cent of the aircraft and crews with which Bomber Command had set out at the start of the year.

The German High Command had jubilantly forecast that casualties on this massive scale would very shortly bring an end to mass attacks by the British. The RAF did not think so, even if their crews did. There was no cheering and little light-hearted chaff at the Bomber Command briefings for Nuremberg. Awaiting the crews that night was a strong and well-organized opposition which had tasted its full share of blood.

The disposition of the night fighters of the Luftwaffe at 30 March was:

	Single-engine night fighters	Twin-engine night fighters
Western Front, including Germany north of 49°	222	576
South Germany and Austria	66	42

Of these 288 single-engine fighters and 618 twin-engine fighters—a total of 906 aircraft—only a small proportion were still operating under the *Himmelbett* system from boxes in the Kammhuber Line.

The majority of aircraft in the German force were greatly improved versions of the twin-engine Junkers Ju 88 and Messerschmitt Me 110, plus the new Heinkel 219, operating as both controlled and non-controlled *zahme Sau* fighters with airbone interception radar and operators and engaged in the long-range pursuit and interception of enemy bombers to and from the target.

About a fifth of the force were Focke-Wulfe 190 and Messerschmitt Me 109 single-engine *wilde Sau* fighters which had first been brought into action at night to attack the incoming bombers over the target area where the glare of searchlights, the Pathfinder target-indicating flares and the fierce fires set by stick after stick of incendiary bombs, often created a 'false dawn', with day-fighting conditions of visibility for the defending German fighters, sometimes up to altitudes of 20 000 feet or more.

Originally briefed to remain over the nightmarishly illuminated target area to fight as long as possible, the *wilde Sau* aircraft recruited from the day-fighting units of the Luftwaffe ultimately had their role extended to pursuing their chosen targets out of the target area and on into the darkness and confusion of the homeward-bound bomber stream until they reached the limits of their comparatively restricted fuel endurance. They then landed at the nearest airfield they could find and were hastily refuelled to resume the pursuit. By any standards this was a risky night's work; even an experienced day-fighter pilot baulked at suddenly being rushed into the intricacies of flying a high-performance single-engine fighter on operations at night when his exposure to the black arts of instrument flying was minimal.

Included in the 302 aircraft which were to operate as the Luftwaffe's night-fighter force that night were also 25 illuminator and observer aircraft, loaded with flares with which to strip the cover of darkness from the British bomber stream.

So, as the crews of Bomber Command approached their waiting aircraft—turrets and cockpit canopies polished, tested and fuelled, bombed-up and ammunitioned—with nothing more to do but climb in, strap up, start up, taxi out, line up and take off far to the west of Nuremberg, the stage for the night's battle was set. All that was lacking was the ultimate illumination: not of radar, searchlights, fires or flares but the moon itself, hanging in the night sky, over a dark and waiting Germany.

By this time General der Flieger Kammhuber was no longer commanding the line of defences which he had created; since November 1943 he had been commander-in-chief, Luftflotte 5, operating over Norway and Finland. However, as the night's events were to prove, the general had trained his men well.

3   The Way In

For Squadron Leader W. L. Brill, DFC, RAAF, this was to be his forty-second operational flight as a pilot and crew captain with Bomber Command. As 'B' Flight commander, No. 463 (RAAF) Squadron, Waddington, Lincolnshire, Brill had no illusions as to what kind of a night he might reasonably expect over Germany.

Right from the moment that he and his crew had walked into the briefing room that evening he sensed that there was something amiss with the planning for the night's operations. An experienced bomber pilot on his second tour of operations over Europe, Brill knew that at this stage of the air war the German night-fighter defences were highly organized, unremittently aggressive and undoubtedly effective. For this reason there were three aspects of the planning for the attack on Nuremberg that he did not like.

First, there was the fact that although the increased efficiency of the Luftwaffe night fighters had forced Bomber Command to operate over Germany only in 'no-moon' periods during the previous twelve months, the RAF would this night be penetrating deep into the heart of Germany in the light of a half-moon.

Secondly, there was the fact that over potentially the most dangerous leg of the planned route—from Position *B*, near Charleroi in enemy-occupied Belgium, to Position *C*, in southern Germany north of Nuremberg, the bomb-heavy, fuel-laden force would be flying a long, straight, undeviating course for two hours.

Thirdly, Squadron Leader Brill did not like the well-intentioned staff planning which had laid on a diversionary ploy of three 'spoof' raids—at Aachen, Cologne and Kassel —on a tangent to the long eastward track of the Main Force bomber stream across the Rhine to Position *C* before the final run-in to Nuremberg.

Brill comforted himself with the thought that, although there was a moon that night, it would be well down in the west and therefore behind the bombers on their long eastward run to Nuremberg past the threat of the German night fighters. This would at least give the rear-gunners and the mid-upper gunners of the Lancasters and Halifaxes a chance to see the night fighters as they approached and attacked from astern which was their usual tactic. It was always nice, Brill thought cynically, to be able to see what was shooting you down.

Privately, Brill reflected that the decision to operate over Germany that night, under half-moon conditions and on a deep penetration target, was contrary to the policy imposed upon Bomber Command by the renewed aggressiveness of the night fighters of the Luftwaffe. Certainly, window would be showered along the route so that the German ground radar stations and the airborne radar set operators in their night fighters would be unable to select individual aircraft targets, but the enemy would still be able to plot the path of the British bomber stream. With its heading established, the German fighters could then be fed in at the tail of the stream like speed-boats in a river.

(Unknown to Brill, of course, and to his colleagues and superiors in Bomber Command, the Luftwaffe had largely overcome the disrupting effect of window's radar-swamping by devising a technique of identifying the electronic emissions from H2S, the terrain-revealing, 'instant-television' radar which the RAF was by now using to locate, mark and bomb targets even through ten-tenths cloud.)

Risking collision with the British bombers and defensive fire from their waiting air gunners, the fighters would fly right through the dense, weaving stream of Lancasters and Halifaxes, picking off targets as they came upon them in the darkness. To Brill it seemed little short of crazy even to have

20

Halifax III E-EASY of No. 462 (RAAF) Squadron over the tranquil English
countryside

'Roger's Lodger'—a Halifax III of No. 466 (RAAF) Squadron, Driffield,
Yorkshire.   *Squadron Leader F. G. Doak, RAAF*

Bomb-doors open, Pilot Officer Lloyd's Lancaster VN-F, of No. 50 Squadron, Skellingthorpe, Lincolnshire, stands at dispersal, awaiting the next operation.
From the Garbett/Goulding Collection, copyright: D. S. Richardson

A ground-staff member of No. 50 Squadron, Skellingthorpe, Lincolnshire, stands below the nose of Pilot Officer Lloyd's Lancaster VN-F—better known to its crew as 'Phyllis Dixey'.
From the Garbett/Goulding Collection, copyright: D. S. Richardson

the force fly a straight leg for two hours through an area of Germany where night-fighter opposition was known, by bitter experience, to be capable of a high intensity of reaction. That, alone, was bad enough.

But to Brill the planning of the three spoof raids on a course tangential to this—the most dangerous section of the bombers' route—could only spell trouble. As he saw it, studying the planned diversion, the night fighters from north-west Germany and the enemy-occupied lowland countries would be attracted to the initial spoof at Aachen. Quickly they would recognize it for what it was—as nothing more than a feint, and then join the bomber stream further to the south. Similarly, the night fighters from Luftwaffe units patrolling in defence of the Ruhr would be attracted by the second spoof at Cologne and then be fed by their ground controllers onto the course of the main stream of British bombers. Finally, the night fighters standing in defence of the 'Big City', Berlin, would be drawn to the third spoof at Kassel, with its aircraft plants and locomotive-building works; having unmasked it as a fake, they would be directed onto the British bomber stream already being pursued by their colleagues from bases in north-western Germany, the Ruhr and in occupied Holland and Belgium.

Brill was so concerned about the undeviating straightness of the leg from Position *B* to Position *C*, and the risks inherent in the adjacent spoof diversions, that he drew in big meat choppers on this section of the route as plotted on the chart of his navigator, Flying Officer E. R. Freeman, RAAF. Jestingly, but not without quiet emphasis, Brill warned his crew that they would have to be alert to slip past underneath the German 'choppers' which would be held in readiness that night.

Since it seemed obvious to Brill that the night's operations had been planned on the basis that there would be sufficient cloud cover to overcome the risk of illumination by the revealing light of the half-moon, he was at least thankful that the meteorologists of Bomber Command had forecast cloud cover all the way across Belgium, France and Germany to Nuremberg with clear bombing weather over the target itself—a commendably co-operative prediction, from the crews' point of view. However, as Brill later recalled, the forecasting data was 'painfully meagre and in the event we had a cloudless run to within twenty miles of the target and then encountered cloud at up to 15 000–20 000 feet over the target.'

When Brill took off from Waddington that night in his Lancaster JO-K there was a small amount of cloud overhead in Lincolnshire but this soon cleared as they flew south to the Channel coast and, by the time they had reached Position *B* near Charleroi, the weather was, as Brill sardonically put it, 'delightfully clear'.

As Brill was later to recall, 'All went well until we had settled down on the long leg from Position *B* to Position *C* but before we were abeam of Aachen the rot had really begun to set in. For the next ninety minutes the bomber stream was continuously under pressure from fighters. It seemed to me that during this entire period I could, at any one time, see three of our aircraft falling in flames. Cannon tracer could be seen in almost every direction—and if it were cannon it was certainly not ours because we did not carry such armament.

'In practically every instance, following a burst of cannon-fire, one of our bombers exploded or began to burn. Some aircraft blew up within fairly close range whilst one or two flew past in flames from stem to stern. The incendiaries from the many doomed aircraft spread over a large area of the ground below and almost the entire track on this leg was traced out in a carpet of burning white incendiaries.

'The cannon-fire being thrown around seemed to be in three colours—white, red and green—and these apparently slowly floating balls of light formed what, under other circumstances, would have been pretty patterns. However, there was one thing about the tracer which did puzzle me. Although I saw dozens of our aircraft being shot down, on only one occasion did I see any return tracer fire from the bombers. This was hard to understand as we were flying down moon. I decided then and there that the night fighters were using upward firing cannon. This was later confirmed when the RAF captured a night fighter and found that it was equipped with two 30-millimetre cannon fixed at an angle from the vertical.* It was merely a matter of: find the quarry, close in from underneath which was in the bomber's blind area, press the trigger and roll clear.'

Apart from tactical innovations such as *Schrage Musik,* the bomber stream was also having to cope with weather which was not behaving as forecast.

'The forecast winds were a little astray,' Squadron Leader Brill recalled. 'The force, or what was left of it, ended up north of track at turning point *C.* The tendency was for all crews to turn near Fulda, north of and short of *C,* and this had some dire results. The searchlights and flak of Schweinfurt came into operation and, to many crews, it seemed to lie where Nuremberg ought to have been. The moment one anxious crew loosed its load on Schweinfurt some dozens followed suit. The previous hour-and-a-half had been enough inducement for anyone to want to unburden his aircraft of the bomb-load as soon as possible and it could well have been that many crews knew they were not over Nuremberg.'

Brill and his crew, however, pressed on to the south, leaving Schweinfurt to their right.

'About twenty miles from Nuremberg,' said Brill, 'we ran into heavy cloud, some of which appeared to tower over 20 000 feet. However, through a small break we could see incendiaries burning where some crews had attacked a town fifteen miles up the river from Nuremberg. Two or three minutes from the target we came out of the cloud at our level although there was still complete cloud below us. Just as we came out of the cloud there was a violent explosion immediately ahead of us.'

For Brill and his crew the target run at Nuremberg was to prove memorable.

If Squadron Leader Brill had had his doubts during the Waddington briefing about the likely outcome of the night's operations, another Australian, Flying Officer D. E. Girardau,

---

*The system was given the German code-name *Schrage Musik*—*Jazz Music*—because its effect was to make the bombers 'dance'. The night-fighter pilot aimed through a reflector sight in the cockpit roof above and in front of him. The upward-firing cannon, usually 20 mm, were set to an angle between 70° and 80°, depending upon the pilot's preference. So that the night fighter could maintain the advantage of surprise for as long as possible while formating below the bomber, the *Schrage Musik* cannon were not loaded with tracer ammunition.

in a No. 4 Group briefing room at RAF Station, Melbourne, further north in Yorkshire, was no more optimistic.

Girardau was the rear gunner of an experienced Halifax crew in 'B' Flight, No. 10 Squadron, RAF, and the only Australian in this typically mixed crew. The mid-upper gunner was a Canadian, Pilot Officer D. Johnson; the wireless air gunner was a Londoner, Pilot Officer Frank Harvey; the flight engineer was a Welshman, Flying Officer Geoff Fenton; the navigator was a New Zealander, Pilot Officer J. Whiteman; the pilot was from Northern Ireland and, curiously, the only non-commissioned member of the crew— Warrant Officer J. T. Clarke.

For Flying Officer Girardau the Nuremberg operation had begun with reporting to the gunnery section of No. 10 Squadron where he was told that the squadron was on call for operations that night. Cycling around the perimeter track to 'B' Flight dispersal he located the new aircraft which had been allocated to his crew. It was a Halifax Mark III with the red identification letters ZA-L straddling the RAF roundels on the matt black sides of the fuselage. Since it was a new aircraft, Girardau decided to carry out a more than usually thorough inspection of his rear turret and its four .303 Browning machine guns.

By 1900 that day, Girardau was waiting with his crew, and the rest of the No. 10 Squadron crews called for operations, in the main briefing room at RAF Melbourne.

When the squadron commander, Wing Commander D. Bradford, RAF, uncovered the big wall map to reveal that the target was Nuremberg, Girardau's crew looked at each other. They had mixed feelings about Nuremberg. The last time they had attacked this city, on the night of 27 August 1943, they had been caught in the cold blue glare of a radar-controlled master searchlight on the way past Frankfurt-am-Main and had been coned by a concentration of 'slave' searchlights for seventeen minutes while Paddy Clarke, their Warrant Officer skipper, had taken violent and seemingly endless evasive action. They had escaped without being shot down but had lost their bomb-aimer, a victim of the ferocity of the Frankfurt defences, and Clarke had had to belly-land the Halifax at Manston, the big emergency airfield in Kent where the North Foreland stands guard over the confluence of the Straits of Dover and the wide and windy approaches to the Thames Estuary.

Now they were going to Nuremberg again, a long and dreary journey at the best. Admittedly there would be a night fighter's moon but there would also be nine-tenths cloud cover for most of the eight-hour flight. Girardau's crew were glad to hear it. This attack against Nuremberg would be the last of their tour of operations: if they walked away from this one they would have beaten the odds that had been the undoing of so many other crews who had started with them and were now long gone.

In Bomber Command, if there was one trip in a tour of thirty operations which was more significant than the first—which so many fresh new crews did not survive—it was surely the last. Girardau's crew were hoping that theirs would be a quiet one with the 'Reaper' looking the other way.

There were eleven other Halifax crews from No. 10 Squadron on the battle-order for that night, with one other crew on stand-by. By 1915, the squadron's crews were out at their dispersals where owls hooted in the nearby woods. Torches flashed as the airmen assembled by the dark, reared bulk of their Halifaxes. After final checks on this fingers-crossed occasion of the last trip, Girardau's crew was ready and at 2000, Warrant Officer Clarke, with his crew of officers from a cross-section of British Empire countries, was taxiing out of his dispersal onto the perimeter track. By 2005, the Halifax was rumbling down the flare-path on take-off from Melbourne with the navigator, Pilot Officer Whiteman, RNZAF, still mindful of the earnestness with which his crew had admonished him to 'keep his finger out'.

The weather was 'very fine' with what seemed to Girardau, in his rear turret, to be almost a full moon. From this vulnerable and conspicuous position with nothing between him and an enemy fighter but his four .303 Brownings and some clear perspex, Girardau could be excused for not seeing much difference between a half-moon and nearly a full moon. Crossing the French coast at 22 000 feet he could see no sign of the cloud cover that the meteorologists had promised: there was no cloud in sight at all.

'The trip to the target was uneventful for us,' Girardau recalled. 'However, on numerous occasions I reported to the skipper that there were many flares in the sky behind us, much more so than on previous trips and I suggested that the Germans were using many 'scarecrows'* this night'.

Later that night, Girardau was to realize that the scarecrows he had watched the Germans firing apparently so prodigiously into the path of the bomber stream had, in fact, actually been RAF bombers exploding. Staring astern from the dark confines of his turret, Girardau had had a grandstand view of the start of the air battle. Since No. 10 Squadron was in the first wave of bombers, and was on time, Halifax ZA-L arrived over the target before the Luftwaffe reaction had reached its full fury.

Still to come, though, was the moment of truth over the target. The bombing run, Girardau remembers, was normal —until Flying Officer Geoff Fenton, the bomb-aimer from Manchester, had dropped his bombs.

Back in England, south of Melbourne, at Skellingthorpe in Lincolnshire, not far from where Squadron Leader Brill had prepared his crew for what looked like being a dicey night, another crew had been confronting the same, somewhat traumatic experience as had Girardau's crew—the last trip of a long and gruelling tour of operations over Europe.

The Skellingthorpe airmen were the crew of Lancaster VN-N in 'B' Flight of No. 50 Squadron, in No. 5 Group. Typically, they were a mixed lot—three Australians in the dark-blue battledress of the RAAF: Pilot Officer D. A. Jennings, pilot and crew captain; Warrant Officer W. C. Hughes, wireless air gunner; Flight Sergeant B. J. F. X. Hayes, mid-upper gunner; and in the grey-blue battledress of the RAF, three Englishmen: Pilot Officer T. Carroll, navigator; Flight Sergeant H. Turton, bomb aimer; Flight Sergeant A. C. Matthews, rear gunner; and lone Scotsman, Flight Sergeant J. Stevens, flight engineer.

---

*Scarecrows were a product of the ingenious minds of the German psychological warfare specialists—they were flak shells which, on bursting, simulated an exploding British bomber complete with blazing, dripping petroleum, flares and signal cartridges. The effect was realistic enough to startle and dismay inexperienced new crews.

As Pilot Officer Jennings and his crew had volunteered for duty with the Pathfinder Force, and this was to be their last trip with No. 50 Squadron, they were less concerned about the dangers of flying one more operation with the Main Force than with signing off from their old squadron with a suitable flourish.

The Australian mid-upper gunner, Flight Sergeant Hayes, noticed nothing significant about the reaction of No. 50 Squadron's crews to the briefing for Nuremberg. If anything there was a noticeable lack of the muttering and uneasy stirring which customarily greeted briefings for the traditionally tougher targets of the 'Big City' or 'Happy Valley'. Even the weather forecast for clear skies and moonlight did not unduly disturb the crew of VN-N. Wise in the ways of the night bomber stream they were as much aware of the risk of collision by darkness as the peril of night fighters in the light of the moon. Combat was something you could do something about but collision was virtually an act of God which came suddenly and apocalyptically upon you.

After briefing, Hayes and his crew shared a comparatively relaxed meal and at dispersal clambered out of the dark, crowded confusion of the crew truck with no great feeling of strain and certainly no presentiment of trouble. If anything, they were elated at having, to this point anyway, completed their tour with No. 50 Squadron, pleased with the prospect of leave and eager to join the elite ranks of the Pathfinder Force.

High above the concrete of the dark Skellingthorpe dispersal, in the cockpit of VN-N, Pilot Officer Jennings and his flight engineer, Jock Stevens, started the four Merlin engines. Together, they began running through their routine checks.

Mainly, it looked like being a long trip, a typical deep penetration attack—at least eight hours according to their navigator, Pilot Officer Carroll. In all that time a lot could happen before they tumbled thankfully back into bed again at Skellingthorpe.

Take-off, climb-out and the crossing of the North Sea to Position *A* were routine, but Flight Sergeant Hayes, from his vantage point in the plastic bubble of the mid-upper turret, quickly noticed how discernible were other bombers in the stream as the moon rose higher.

'In fact I had never before been able to see so many of our aircraft so clearly at night,' he said. 'Crossing the enemy coast was uneventful and we had penetrated deep into enemy territory before the first alarms began. These were in the form of large red splashes on the ground caused by falling aircraft, and tracers in the sky. By this time we were about thirty minutes away from the target and first enemy aircraft sighting occurred about this time.'

The sighting was to be far from the last that night for young Brian Hayes and his crew.

Earlier that night, north of Skellingthorpe at Binbrook, on the Humber, south-west of Grimsby, Australians of No. 460 (RAAF) Squadron, in No. 1 Group, had also been getting ready to go to Nuremberg. Amongst them was Flight Sergeant J. G. Earl, navigator in the crew of Lancaster P-PETER, flown by Flight Lieutenant D. Donaldson, from Brighton, Melbourne, Australia.

It was the crew's seventh operation.

Crouched over his chart table for eight hours and fifteen minutes of navigation in the cramped tunnel of the Lancaster's fuselage, John Earl had little time for looking at the scenery on the way into Nuremberg.

All that he was able to recall of that lurid night of flame and tracer was that after P-PETER crossed the Belgian coast into enemy territory—where the forecast ten-tenths cloud cover dispersed to leave an open sky—the crew experienced night-fighter attacks throughout the whole journey.

'The volume of attacks was considerably greater than we had experienced on any other trip,' he said.

For another Australian in No. 460 Squadron, Pilot Officer C. P. 'Paddy' Gundelach, a pilot in 'B' Flight, the Nuremberg operation was notable mainly for the fact that it was the second trip of his first tour of operations.

With him in his Lancaster M-MIKE was a rather diverse crew for an Australian squadron such as No. 460. It comprised: a New Zealand navigator, Warrant Officer 'Mac' McFarlane; a Canadian bomb aimer, Flying Officer Dough Williams; a Canadian rear gunner, Flight Sergeant

Bill Rendall; an RAF flight engineer, Sergeant 'Red' Akers; an RAF wireless air gunner, Flight Sergeant Tommy Tucker; and an RAF mid-upper gunner, Sergeant Ray Warton.

Gundelach recalls that, to the best of his memory, the Nuremberg briefing at Binbrook was attended by Group Captain H. I. Edwards VC, the station commander at Binbrook, and Wing Commander H. D. 'Spike' Marsh, commanding officer, No. 460 Squadron.

'I am not sure whether either of these officers operated that night,' Gundelach said. 'However, as a point of interest I noticed during my tour that if Group Captain Edward's name was on the battle-order for an operation it was never a piece of cake.'

Certainly Nuremberg was not destined to be placed in such a category.

Gundelach was able to remember little of the way to the target that night except that his windscreen iced up as he climbed to height before setting course for Position *A* over the North Sea between the coasts of East Anglia and of Belgium. Despite the moonlight, now unobscured by cloud, Gundelach and his crew managed to reach the target without being attacked by enemy fighters. Such was the luck of the game in Bomber Command—a freshman crew like Paddy Gundelach's sailing through unintercepted to Nuremberg, while experienced, combat-wise crews had had to slug it out in the face of repeated attacks.

In contrast to Gundelach's crew, Pilot Officer S. A. Moorhouse, RAAF, and his crew, also of 'B' Flight, had the benefit of considerably more operational experience with which to confront the enemy forces that would be disposed in defence of Nuremberg that night.

For Pilot Officer Moorhouse, a navigator, and his crew—Pilot Officer R. Howell, RAAF, pilot; Flight Sergeant N. Lukies, RAAF, bomb aimer; Flight Sergeant C. Jewitt, RAF, flight engineer; Flight Sergeant L. Field, wireless air gunner; Flight Sergeant 'Bluey' Hill, RAAF, mid-upper gunner; and Flight Sergeant W. Shaw, RAF, rear gunner—this would be their twenty-third operation. They were well on their way to completing their tour of operations, but once their Lancaster L-LOVE was airborne Pilot Officer Moorhouse would have little time for the luxury of worrying about chances of survival.

As the crew's navigator he would be responsible not only for seeing to it that his aircraft stayed on track for the better part of eight hours over blacked-out Europe but also for computing wind velocities encountered during the trip to be broadcast back to base. Like all the navigators manning the aircraft of Bomber Command that night, Moorhouse could at best look forward to a long night of exhaustive responsibility and hard work with little or no opportunity to see what was happening outside the red glow of the light over his plotting table.

Take-off for L-LOVE was at 2157.

From Position *B* near Charleroi the heading was due east as Moorhouse remembers it.

'From the turning point until some distance east of Frankfurt (the route passed about thirty miles north of Frankfurt) fighter activity and flak were very heavy,' he said. 'Whilst we were not hit or attacked, the gunners and the pilot saw many falling aircraft in this corridor area.'

The night was to be memorable for another navigator, Canadian J. F. Maxwell of No. 97 Pathfinder squadron, based at Bourn, near Cambridge. He and his crew were flying as primary target markers, taking with them ten Parramatta and Wanganui flares in the bomb bay of their Lancasters.

'In perspective', said Maxwell, 'the whole operation was a disaster. Our particular aircraft, first out on the raid with the Pathfinder Force, was engaged by enemy aircraft upon reaching the French coast. At this time I took our aircraft ten miles port of track for some illogical reason and held this position until the target area. The gunners reported numerous combats to starboard all along the route, which lead us to believe the route was known beforehand by the Luftwaffe.

'Another strange thing about this raid was that, upon engagement by enemy aircraft, our guns would not fire. This was reported by other aircraft that returned from the trip, leading us to believe that a combination of climatic conditions and humidity affected the .303 calibre guns of the Lancaster aircraft participating. This was the first and last time this occurred in the fifty-six trips that I carried out with the Pathfinders.'

Among the experienced airmen briefed for Nuremberg was the crew captained by Wing Commander F. W. Thompson, DFC, AFC, of No. 44 Squadron at Dunholme Lodge, about ten miles north of Lincoln.

It was an entirely English crew: Wing Commander Thompson, about 27, was from Blackpool; the navigator, Flight Sergeant A. Stancer, 22, was from London where he had been an office worker; the bomb aimer, Flying Officer Bill Clegg, 25, a former bank clerk, was from Manchester as was the wireless operator, Pilot Officer Pete Roberts, 23, who had worked in an office; the mid-upper gunner, Flight Sergeant Middleham, 23, had been a factory-hand in Leeds; and the rear gunner, Flight Sergeant J. Hall, was a former Yorkshire mill-hand.

Despite a diversity of background the crew had one thing in common other than their nationality—their operational experience.

The briefing at Dunholme Lodge began at 2000.

'This was indeed a "maximum effort" being deep in enemy territory,' recalled Burrows, 'and the memory of a raid similar to this (Leipzig) where we lost seventy-nine aircraft was fresh in our minds.'

Since Thompson, Burrows, Middleham and Hall were on their second tour of operations with well over fifty trips each to Germany behind them, and Stancer, Roberts and Clegg had each flown about twelve, the crew's remarks about the choice of Nuremberg as a target were pointed, to say the least. (Subsequent to the Nuremberg operation, Middleham, Stancer and Hall were to be posted missing, believed killed.)

As Burrows saw it, the Wing Commander's briefing for Nuremberg was a routine affair. On a large map of Germany were displayed the defended areas marked according to their strength and nature—flak in red, searchlights in blue, and fighter areas indicated by small aircraft symbols.

'As various crews entered and glanced at the map, the usual

"Cor! Bloody hell!" remarks filled the air, especially as the target was shown deep in enemy territory,' said Burrows. 'My own reaction to all this was the usual butterfly tummy, especially due to the fact that we, being the most experienced crew, had been detailed to take photographs and assess bombing after doing our own bombing run. This mission obviously meant hanging around the target far too long for comfort, having to run backwards and forwards and being bombed from above by our own aircraft (which incidentally had happened before, having had incendiary bombs in the wing) and the usual flak and night fighters being assisted by the bright lights.'

After the briefing the crews, already dressed in their flying gear, were taken by crew bus out to their aircraft dispersals. 'They were unusually quiet this particular night,' said Burrows.

Each crew was dropped at its aircraft with a 'Good luck! Have a good trip.' from the WAAF driver. Burrows' crew being what their driver called her 'ace' crew, were delivered last so that she could stay around while they carried out their ground checks and smoked their last cigarettes. Despite a standing Bomber Command order forbidding it, Burrows 'spent' his usual superstitious nervous 'penny' by the port wheel; after that they were ready to go. Their Lancaster, KM-Z, Serial Number ND 515, was loaded with approximately 10 000 pounds of bombs including one 4000-pound high-explosive 'cookie' and approximately 6000 pounds of incendiaries.

Sitting in the same briefing room as Flying Officer 'Gerry' Girardau at No. 10 Squadron, Melbourne, Yorkshire, was another Australian, Flying Officer F. R. Stuart. There was actually no need for him to be there as his crew had already completed its tour of operations on Halifaxes with No. 10 Squadron. They had been 'screened' from operational flying but Stuart had not relished the prospect of returning to a training unit to fly as a tour-expired gunnery instructor— inevitably with crews under training—so he had elected to remain on operational flying with No. 10 Squadron.

On this occasion, Stuart had been put on the battle-order

to fly as a 'spare bod' gunner with an all-RAF crew. In view of his operational experience he would be flying in the mid-upper turret as fire controller.

Stuart's night over Nuremberg began when he reported to the squadron's gunnery leader, Squadron Leader G. Lowe, DFC, after returning from leave in London.

George Lowe—better known to the air gunners of No. 10 Squadron as 'Jarge'—had already completed one tour of operations. A cheerfully cynical type he had grinned when Stuart asked him if there was anything doing because if there wasn't Stuart intended dodging off to his quarters for a recuperative sleep after his London leave and the long trip in the slow, crowded train back to Yorkshire.

Squadron Leader Lowe had sat back in his chair, closed one eye in a conspiratorial wink and said, 'I think you'd like to be on this one. It's a DP'. For Stuart there was to be no sleeping that day nor until dawn of the next day: he was on the squadron battle-order to fly this deep-penetration attack with a new crew.

After checking with the station intelligence section to see if the Luftwaffe had introduced new fighting tactics, or any other tricks, Stuart went out to his crew's Halifax M-MIKE, and began checking and harmonizing the two Browning .303 machine-guns in the mid-upper turret while the rest of the crew busied themselves with their own checks of equipment and armament.

Stuart had often flown in M-MIKE and liked the aircraft. He was reassured but not surprised when the battle-tried Halifax responded to all the demands put upon her by their keen young pilot during the course of a routine night-flying test in the squadron's local flying area. After they had landed, taxied back to dispersal and left the aircraft for the ground staff to re-fuel and bomb up, the day began to move faster.

Stuart settled into the usual routine with which he had become so familiar, and which had so sustained him during his tour of operations—the hasty meal, the checking of oxygen masks and intercom and, in the case of the gunners, the bright yellow, electrically heated Taylorsuits. These were designed to keep them warm and therefore alert in their draughty, unpressurised turrets, far from the heating system which served the cockpit and navigation stations in the aircraft. Sometimes, of course, the electric flying suits did not work and the result was a night of seemingly endless misery. Then there was the quick nap, if possible.

For Stuart, there was his own private ritual which he always observed before going out on an operation. The shower and the shave. Then, for warmth during the forthcoming night's work, silk underwear next to his skin. Then the RAF-issue lambswool underwear topped by a clean shirt and his battledress. Last came a pair of silk stockings which he wore as an inner flying scarf. A jaunty gesture to the dashing traditions of the Royal Flying Corps, the stockings were valued more for the luck they had brought during a tour of operations than the charms of their original wearer, a London actress.

At No. 10 Squadron's main briefing there was the usual air of tense expectancy until the big target map was uncovered by the station's 'chief spy'. There was no need for the intelligence officer to point out the target. The big, blood-red button was in position—Nuremberg, parade-ground of the Nazi Party and brewer of strong Bavarian beer. After the customary warnings about searchlights, flak and fighters, according to the RAF's current intelligence summaries of the German defences, the crews drew their parachutes, cracked the usual jokes with the parachute section WAAFs, lashed up their Mae West life-jackets and climbed aboard the crew buses which would take them out to the dispersals.

Stuart remembers that there was the usual cynical chaffing and ribaldry between the crews as they climbed out of the buses and dumped their miscellany of gear by their aircraft. Morale had always been high in No. 10 Squadron and on this occasion it was entirely undiminished by any implicit threat in the fact that the name of that night's target was Nuremberg.

Take-off in Halifax ZA-M—a 'cleaned-up', higher-performance Mark III version with radial engines—was normal, as was the rendezvous with Main Force over the North Sea and the inevitable greeting of flak as they crossed the enemy coast of occupied Belgium.

Then Stuart saw the first British aircraft going down.

'Hell, the fighters are up already,' the skipper's voice rasped over the intercom. 'It looks as if they're waiting for us. Gunners, test your guns and everyone keep a sharp lookout.'

By this time Stuart and the rear gunner needed little admonition.

'We had barely finished testing our guns,' said Stuart, 'when a Ju 88 fired at us from the beam at about a hundred yards range. A quick burst from our guns in reply seemed to deter him and he presumably went off in search of easier prey. I remember saying to the skipper that I didn't like the look of things and that it could be a really sticky night. This proved to be somewhat of an understatement as we had more combats before we reached the target area. Both of these attacks were pressed home with vigour, courage, skill and determination and I can assure you that we were glad when they broke off their attacks. Heavily laden though she was, M-MIKE had behaved like a thoroughbred.'

The target was still to come.

Far to the south of Melbourne, Yorkshire, that night, at Wyton, a Pathfinder base in Huntingdonshire, another Australian mid-upper gunner had also sat and listened to the briefing for Nuremberg. He was Warrant Officer A. G. Strickland, from Dromana, a seaside town on Port Phillip Bay, near Melbourne, Australia. He was the only Australian flying with an otherwise all-English crew in Lancaster R-ROGER in 'B' Flight, No. 83 Squadron, No. 8 Pathfinder Group.

Strickland's pilot was Flight Lieutenant Roy Hellier, RAF. The other five RAF members of the crew were: Flying Officer G. Baxter, navigator; Pilot Officer R. Haynes, set operator; Flight Sergeant F. Wildman, flight engineer; Flight Sergeant G. Cassey, wireless air gunner and Flight Sergeant G. Harrison, rear gunner.

Preoccupied as usual with the tactical factors associated with air gunnery, Warrant Officer Strickland noted mainly that the weather forecast indicated the crews could expect cloud cover over most of the route and over the target area.

'In fact', Strickland recalls, 'there was cover for only about two-thirds of the track in, the last third and the target itself was clear. I consider this resultant visibility, together with radar aids, enabled the enemy to track and vector his aircraft onto us. The heavier armament carried by his fighters enabled them to stand off and shoot down our aircraft as their effective range was some two hundred to seven hundred yards in excess of ours.

'Our meteorological forecasts were in error regarding winds and many of our aircraft found, on breaking cloud cover, that they were some twenty to thirty minutes ahead of track. The resultant milling around of some two hundred aircraft gave the enemy some indication as to our target. Again, some of our aircraft (who had failed to check their position after breaking cover) were now approaching Nuremberg and the choice of target was plain to the enemy.'

At Waddington, in Lincolnshire, crews of No. 467 (RAAF) Squadron, which shared the airfield with No. 463 (RAAF) Squadron, were attending the same briefing which had moved Squadron Leader Brill to warn his crew that ahead of them they could expect to have a rough night.

Acting Flight Lieutenant D. T. Conway, RAAF, from Cottesloe, Perth, Western Australia, the pilot of Lancaster K-KING, 'A' Flight, No. 467 Squadron, had one other Australian in his crew—Sergeant McDade, bomb aimer. The other crew positions were held by RAF airmen: Sergeants J. Wesley, navigator; Tanfield, flight engineer; Redman, wireless air gunner; Stone, mid-upper gunner and Day, rear gunner.

The crew was a brotherhood of arms, for the men had flown on nineteen operations together, including six against Berlin, and had survived two major attacks which had taken a heavy toll of the RAF's bomber crews earlier that year— Leipzig on 19 February (with seventy-eight British bombers lost) and, less than a week before this attack on Nuremberg, Berlin on 24 March. Conway had flown an extra trip to Berlin as a second pilot on 16 December 1943, at the start of his tour of operations.

The Nuremberg briefing, Conway noted, was routine except that there was some talk among the crews about this being the first major attack for a long time to penetrate

Two members of the crew of Lancaster AS-K of No. 166 Squadron, of Kirmington, near Grimsby, Lincolnshire—the Russian-born RAAF bomb aimer, Sergeant V. V. Zamiatin (left), and Sergeant S. Lipman, RAF, flight engineer. *V. V. Zamiatin*

From the cockpit of Flight Lieutenant C. J. Ginder's Lancaster ZN-V of No. 106 Squadron, Metheringham, Lincolnshire, the crew's bomb aimer, Flying Officer W. G. Seymour, has good reason to smile on return from Nuremberg— the operation was the last of the crew's tour of duty. *Copyright: W. G. Seymour*

Sergeant R. MacIntosh, in charge of the ground-staff which serviced Flight
Lieutenant C. J. Ginder's Lancaster ZN-V of No. 106 Squadron, Methering-
ham, Lincolnshire, after the aircraft's safe return from Nuremberg.
Copyright: W. G. Seymour

so deeply into Germany so late in the moon period.

'It turned out to be a lovely night with a good moon and no cloud over France,' Conway recalls. 'Approximately south of Aachen the combats began and it was soon obvious that the enemy fighters were out in good strength. I had to warn my crew not to comment on the combats but rather to maintain a good look-out. My engineer did, however, at one stage count seven aircraft falling in flames and a further eleven burning on the ground.

'The fighters seemed to know our course as, when we did alter course, they turned with us. It was at this stage, some twenty minutes before our time-on-target that a series of bright flashes like a giant sparkler appeared close to port. At the same instant both gunners called "Dive port." I think I was already on my way. As the port outer motor was on fire I maintained the dive in the hope that the speed would help extinguish the flames and I also checked that the flight engineer was feathering the airscrew of the correct motor. The fire in the port outer motor went out as I continued rolling the aircraft into the standard corkscrew evasive manoeuvre as we were again under attack by night fighters. Both my gunners were firing back but they observed no hits. The fighter then broke away. About five minutes later we were attacked again but no damage was done. A crew check revealed no injuries and no observable damage to the aircraft apart from the port outer motor. We were now down to about 17 500 feet having been attacked initially at about 21 500 feet. My navigator, Sergeant Joe Wesley, gave me a course for the target where the attack was now developing.'

It took Conway longer to reach the target than its apparent nearness indicated.

'I think it was about this time that the air-speed indicator began to play up', he recalls. 'We had been plagued with icing trouble at the pitot head and on several previous occasions had flown to and from the target with no indicated air speed. This trouble seemed to occur mostly when flying in mist or vapour trails at altitude and we now were in a slight haze.'

Outside in the thin cold air enveloping Conway's Lancaster under the glow of a rising moon, the weather conditions were already becoming ideal for the formation of the tell-tale contrails that were to betray the bomber stream that night.

Conway's navigator, Sergeant Joseph Wesley, formerly a draughtsman from Watford, Hertfordshire, has his own recollections of the way into Nuremberg in Lancaster PO-K:

'After the two previous trips—Berlin and Essen—it was a nice change to have a southerly trip to what for us was a new target,' he said. 'At briefing the met. was fairly favourable as it indicated some cloud cover but this eventually proved to be far from accurate and there was bright moonlight with almost complete lack of cloud. At briefing we had been told about the special marker flares to be used by PFF. These were to be positioned on the way out, off the actual route and were to be falsely indicated turning-points.

'After a satisfactory ground check we got airborne at approximately 2145 with our bomb load of 12 000 pounds on the first leg out across the east coast to a point in the North Sea where we changed course slightly about 10° starboard to cross the enemy coast near Zeebrugge, flying in a south-easterly direction to a point about thirty miles south of Brussels.

'Almost as soon as we crossed the coast we were made aware of the terrific enemy aerial activity which was only too apparent in the sight of bombers bursting into flames.

'As navigator it was part of my duties to record in my log any activity reported by the remainder of the crew—combats, aircraft shot down, with estimated positions.

'Within a very short time the reportage became excessive and we were made positively aware that this was going to be a night to remember.

'We now turned onto an almost easterly course which took us south of Aachen for approximately 240 miles to a position about 70 miles north of the target where we altered course to an almost southerly heading for the target. Just when we were complimenting ourselves on being out of trouble on what we already knew to be a very bad night for the bombers, we were attacked by a Ju 88. Fortunately the gunners were on the job and we counter-attacked, but the Ju 88 persisted. Our pilot took evasive action, really throwing the aircraft around violently but, in spite of this, cannon shells came through the fuselage, without causing serious damage, until the port outer engine was hit and feathered out of action.

'I was beginning to think "this is it" and that our luck was running out when suddenly the attack ended and the Ju 88 disappeared.

' "He's gone" was the most welcome sound and an eternity that had been compressed into minutes was over.'

Not far from Waddington, at Fiskerton, also in Lincolnshire, Flight Sergeant W. F. Morrisby, RAAF, was attending main briefing for the crews of No. 49 Squadron, another unit of No. 5 Group.

Morrisby was flying that night as a 'spare bod' rear gunner with Pilot Officer Clarke's crew in 'B' Flight. As a temporary crew replacement for the night's operations he did not know the crew very well, nor was he even sure of their names. Once airborne, in the rear turret of Clarke's Lancaster EA-U he might well miss the familiar tones of his own regular crew's voices on the intercom but if there was to be action this night then his situation at the tail-end of the aircraft would be no more lonely than it had ever been before.

After the main briefing, Morrisby noticed only that, like himself, many members of No. 49 Squadron's crews commented critically on the long, direct, undeviating section of the route from south of Aachen to the turning-point north-west of Nuremberg. To Morrisby, the planning also seemed unusual because in contrast to previous operations against heavily defended German cities such as Nuremberg, this attack was being carried out during a moon period. As a rear gunner, isolated between the tall, twin fins and rudders of the Lancaster, Morrisby was more than mindful of the implications of the state of the moon.

So far as No. 49 Squadron was concerned, though, there was some consolation in the fact that Fiskerton's Lancasters would be flying in the first wave of the Main Force bomber stream and would therefore be attacking and departing the target before the hornets' nest of the Luftwaffe's night fighters had been stirred up and directed into action by their controllers.

Morrisby recalls that no difficulties were experienced that

night until after crossing the Belgian coast when some sporadic but accurate flak necessitated evasive action. No fighter flares, dropped to illuminate the bomber stream, were observed, nor any attacks.

'From about half way along the leg from Aachen to the turning-point for the target run-in,' Morrisby recalls, 'the position changed radically. German fighters had marked the route very efficiently with flares and this, coupled with the half-moon and cloud below our height of 21 000 feet, tended to silhouette aircraft flying at a lower altitude to a very marked degree. At this stage I observed many combats in the waves following behind us and aircraft falling.'

For Pilot Officer A. R. S. Bowman, RAAF, another pilot of 'A' Flight in No. 463 (RAAF) Squadron, Waddington, and his crew—Sergeant R. L. Seton, RAAF, navigator; Sergeant M. C. J. Barber DFM, RAF, bomb aimer; and the four other English crew members: Sergeant R. E. Clarke, flight engineer; Sergeant L. F. Westgate, wireless air gunner; Sergeant A. C. Wilson, mid-upper gunner and Sergeant F. Dobson, rear gunner—it was something of a relief that they were being briefed for operations only against Nuremberg. Certainly, they were no more worried about this trip than about the eighteen others which they had already completed, including ten to Berlin.

To Bowman it seemed that the meteorological forecast at briefing was satisfactory from an operational point of view even if it meant a considerable amount of instrument flying with so much cloud expected along the route to Nuremberg, clearing to seven-tenths over the target area.

Bowman's bomb-load that night was 10 796 pounds and the all-up weight for take-off in his Lancaster JO-J was 65 400 pounds.

'Soon after we flew over the coast,' he recalled, 'we could see fires on the ground and plenty of enemy night fighters and we soon realized that the fires were our own aircraft that were being shot down one after another. The night turned out to be not only very clear with hardly a cloud but there was almost a full moon and they were waiting for us. I remember saying to my navigator that we did not need his skill that night as one only had to follow the fires (of shot-down aircraft burning on the ground) to keep on track. From this moment on we really had to keep on our toes. It was so clear and it was so easy to see where our other bombers were that I decided that I would alter course as much as possible so as not to be such a sitting duck. Many fighters flew over and under us and we would no sooner get one alert and there would be another, only minutes after. Our gunners had plenty of practice this night and I think, from memory, that they shot up two.'

Unlike Pilot Officer Bowman's philosophic approach towards a target that for once was not Berlin, the night's operations were to be something of an initiation for Flying Officer H. J. Barker DFC, an Australian navigator flying with No. 139 (Jamaica) Squadron, RAF, based at Upwood, Huntingdon-shire.

With his pilot, Flying Officer Allan Brown, RAF, Barker would be both dropping bombs and observing the success or otherwise of the attack.

No. 139 Squadron was at that time being prepared for service as a Pathfinder squadron with Bennett's No. 8 Group.

Barker's aircraft, v-victor, a Mosquito Mark IV, was carrying four 500-pound general-purpose bombs which he would aim at target-indicator flares to be dropped by other Pathfinder Mosquitoes at Nuremberg, ahead of the Main Force stream of Lancasters and Halifaxes. Barker and his English pilot were briefed that after they had bombed on the PFF marker flares they were to circle the target and assess the progress of the attack for as long as possible within the limits of their fuel endurance. For Flying Officers Brown and Barker in their Mosquito there was to be no thankful dash for the concealing obscurity of the darkness beyond the target as soon as their bomb-bay doors closed. As they left the briefing room at Upwood they certainly could not claim that their night was going to be a boring one.

For Flight Sergeant Whitlock, RAAF, a Londoner born in Constantinople, the code words 'Grand National' booming out that morning on the Tannoy public address system at

RAF Station, Kirmington, in No. 1 Group, were to trigger a sequence of events and procedures which, though initially familiar, were to culminate in a night that Sidney Nicholas Whitlock would never forget.

To the Lancaster crews of No. 166 Squadron at Kirmington a broadcast of 'Grand National' echoing in mess halls, hangars, crew-rooms and even in latrines, was a warning that the station had been alerted by No. 1 Group for a 'maximum effort' operation that night.

With the target still unannounced but its imminence confirmed, members of No. 166 Squadron crews immediately began reporting to their respective sections for specialist briefings on the basic information they would need for operations that night, regardless of what target they would be attacking.

While Flight Sergeant Whitlock, wireless air gunner, reported to the signals section, his pilot, Flight Lieutenant F. Taylor, RAF, made his way to the office of his 'A' Flight commander. Simultaneously, the four other RAF crew members were also reporting to their respective sections— Flight Sergeant L. McCarney, the Irish navigator; Flight Sergeant W. Watson, bomb aimer; Sergeant J. Whitfield, flight engineer; Pilot Officer S. Standen, mid-upper gunner and Sergeant F. Thrower, rear gunner.

With the primary specialist briefings completed, Whitlock and his crew cycled thoughtfully out to their dispersal where their ground crew, similarly alerted by the Tannoy's broadcast of 'Grand National', were completing inspection and maintenance of the engines, systems and armament of Lancaster v-victor.

Since night-flying tests prior to operations were not carried out at No. 166 Squadron unless some previously reported defect had been rectified and had to be tested in flight, there was no need for Whitlock and his crew to check-fly v-victor that morning as she had a clean sheet. Instead, while Taylor and Whitfield started the Lancaster's four motors, ran them up, checked flight and engine instruments, the hydraulic, pneumatic and electrical systems, the oxygen system and flight controls, the rest of the crew carried out their own ground tests: Watson, in the nose, checking his bombing panel, bomb sight and front turret; McCarney at his navigation table behind the black-out curtain in the fuselage tunnel aft of the cockpit, checking repeater compass, altimeter, airspeed indicator, radar aids, red plotting light and the sharpness of his plotting pencils; Standen and Thrower checking rotation of their turrets, elevation, depression and cocking of their guns and illumination of their gun-sights; aft of the navigator, Whitlock at his radio station, checking R/T and W/T radio equipment, crew intercom system plugs and microphones, flares, Verey pistol and signal cartridges. Seated before the bright red, green, blue and yellow knurled knobs of his bank of radio equipment, Whitlock carried out no actual test broadcast for, as usual during Bomber Command preparations for an attack, radio silence had been imposed on all squadrons throughout the command lest German signals monitors, across the English Channel, drew obvious conclusions from any sudden and significant increase in radio traffic on Bomber Command frequencies.

With v-VICTOR checked and not found wanting by the men who would fly her on their eighteenth operation, Whitlock and his friends cycled back to billets or mess where the dawdling hours passed slowly, as usual, but with an undeniable relentlessness not to be denied by doing the customary small things of pretended normality—a quiet smoke, a letter to be written, a stroll in the sharp Yorkshire air, a restless nap, a shave, a book chapter to be finished . . . waiting, wondering or, if your faith was still firm, a hasty and apologetic prayer for good luck.

The ops meal when it came was a quickening of relief after the hours of waiting for dull time to pass. Crowded four to a table, the crews ate in an atmosphere alive with young voices raised in animated, nervous chatter and frank, extroverted speculation about the target and their prospects for the night.

Even more of a relief was the main briefing for all members of all crews. If you had been to briefings before then there was nothing particularly different about this one; it was just like all the others which, in itself, was always reassuring. Perhaps the only factor which caused Whitlock's crew to exchange questioning glances was the discovery that they would be flying in the light of a night fighter's moon. Like the rest of the crews of No. 166 Squadron they were consoled, if not cheered, by the fact that the meteorologists had promised them cloud cover. On this basis, then, there would be no great need to worry about the rising moon.

Ironically, Whitlock was to recall clearly that, shortly after v-VICTOR had completed the North Sea crossing and was over Belgium, he heard his pilot, Taylor, and the gunners reporting that the little cloud that had been around was rapidly breaking up.

The consequences were not long in coming.

'A few minutes after listening to the Group broadcast at midnight,' said Whitlock, 'a fighter put a burst into the belly of the aircraft, having come up from the pitch black below. The aircraft rocked, my set started smoking and the aircraft started filling with smoke. The R/T was dead, transmitter and receiver out of action and not a sound on the intercom. The navigator and bomb aimer came back to me and pointed to the rear of the aircraft, indicating it was time to leave. By this time flame was spouting through the inspection panels and acrid smoke had filled the aircraft. Getting the mid-upper gunner down from his turret, we made for the rear entrance door of the aircraft, on the starboard side, where we found that the rear gunner had already jettisoned the door. On our approach he left the aircraft followed by the mid-upper gunner. I was next and on looking around was aghast to see the navigator with his parachute canopy opened and spilled out, having caught his rip-cord handle on part of the mid-upper turret mounting. I then left the aircraft and as I floated down flames were streaming from the bomb-bay of the aircraft. Landing with a breathtaking jolt I found the ground covered in light snow.'

Another member of No. 166 Squadron, Sergeant Sidney Lipman, RAF, a flight engineer from London, in 'B' Flight, had also heard the 'Grand National' alert on the Tannoy at Kirmington.

With his crew, Lipman had joined No. 166 Squadron less than two weeks earlier. They had arrived on 8 March from Feltwell where they had undergone a week's conversion course on Lancasters having originally trained on Stirlings, the four-engined bombers which by then had been phased out of operations with Bomber Command. Returning to Kirmington from leave on 26 March, Lipman was asked if he would like to fly on operations that evening with another crew as they were short of a flight engineer. Being keen to get to know the Lancaster as quickly and thoroughly as possible, he agreed to go. With a crew skippered by Flight Sergeant Fransden he went to Essen that night where, for the first time, he experienced accurately directed flak. No. 166 Squadron lost two Lancasters that night.

A few days later, on the afternoon of 30 March, the enthusiastic young Sergeant Lipman was again called to the 'B' Flight commander's office and asked if he would fly another 'guest' trip with a crew whose flight engineer was ill.

With unconscious humour, Sidney Lipman recalls that 'I felt that it was extremely nice of them to think of me and said I would be pleased to go. I was told that I would fly with Flight Lieutenant Proctor who introduced himself to me and was a very affable type of person. I inspected and checked over the aircraft, petrol gauges, flaps, etcetera, and found everything perfect.

'Later on we went to the briefing room where we were given all the gen about the raid and what to expect in the way of enemy resistance and were wished the best of luck by "Pop," the briefing officer. As we were leaving the briefing room a chap came over to Flight Lieutenant Proctor and spoke to him and then they both came over to me. Proctor said that the fellow was his own flight engineer who had been given an all-clear by the MO and would like to fly on this trip if I had no objection. I said that as long as the CO did not mind I would be quite willing to forgo the trip. After putting it to the CO it was agreed that he would take my place. I wished them luck.'

(Wherever possible, Bomber Command was reluctant to break up or separate crews whose members, naturally, flew best with those they knew best. Unlike an American B17 Flying Fortress or B24 Liberator crew, the members of a Bomber Command crew flew every trip of their tour of operations together, regardless of rank or crew station.)

At this early stage of his operational career young Lipman had not yet actually watched the station's aircraft taking off on operations so he now availed himself of the opportunity to do so from out by the runway. He was enjoying the spectacle of Lancaster after Lancaster of the squadron howling off, black-bellied, into the darkness when he felt a firm but friendly hand on his shoulder.

It was the commanding officer of No. 166 Squadron.

'You're just the chap I wanted to see,' the Wing Commander said. 'One of the flight engineers is not well. Unless his crew can get another engineer they will be unable to go on this op. Can you help us out? Of course, you have the right to refuse.'

By then, as Lipman puts it, he no longer fancied the trip but although his heart said no, he agreed to go. The Wing Commander, naturally enough, was delighted.

'He whipped me off to the parachute section in his car,' 'Lipman recalled, ' ran me back to the runway where a kite was revving-up and helped me into the open door of the aircraft. I then met my pilot, Pilot Officer Bridges, took my place alongside him and off we went.'

It is not difficult to imagine the zeal with which the young flight engineer was propelled into the night's forthcoming air battle since nothing was more the bane of a squadron commander's life than an aborted take-off.

Lipman's was the last Lancaster from No. 166 Squadron to take off, the last to get a green 'go' flashed by Aldis lamp from the plastic bowl in the roof of the black-and-yellow-striped 'pie-cart' near the threshold of the runway.

If Flight Sergeant Sidney Lipman could be said to have been press-ganged away from his own crew and onto the Nuremberg operation it must also be said that it was done in the nicest possible way and largely as a result of his readily demonstrated enthusiasm at a time when a bloody-nosed Bomber Command needed all the enthusiasm it could get.

With his host pilot for the night, Pilot Officer Bridges, in a Lancaster III, z-zebra, Lipman found himself crossing the enemy coast again but without being troubled by flak. On the route towards Nuremberg he noted what appeared to be many enemy aircraft. Approaching the target area he saw some Bomber Command aircraft shot down, but by flak, not night fighters.

Earlier in the day, at Leconfield in Yorkshire, north of the windy Humber with the balloon-barrages that guarded the busy port of Hull, Flight Sergeant Harry 'Spider' Webb, RAF, from Sketchley Hall, Hinckley, Leicestershire, saw his crew's names listed on the squadron readiness board at 1100. Harry was a mid-upper gunner in D-DOG, a Halifax Mark III, of 'A' Flight, No. 640 Squadron, No. 4 Group, a sister squadron of No. 466 (RAAF) Squadron. Checking over the guns, the gun sight and the hydraulic system of his mid-upper turret, Webb was not to know how much he would be needing his guns that night—or the knuckle-bruising trouble he would experience with them.

With his crew—Flight Sergeant Johnson, RAF, pilot; Flight Sergeant Hancock, RAF, navigator; Flying Officer Laine, RCAF, bomb aimer; Sergeant Mitchell, RAF, flight engineer; Sergeant Smith, RAF, wireless air gunner and Flight Sergeant Ellis, RCAF, rear gunner—Webb attended No. 640 Squadron's main briefing at 1500. There they learned that the target was Nuremberg and that they would be attacking with the second wave of the main bomber stream, assembling for rendezvous over the Wash before setting course for the enemy coast.

After what Harry recalls as 'the last supper'—his squadron's sardonic description of the crews' pre-operational meal—Flight Sergeant Johnson lifted Halifax D-DOG off the Leconfield runway at 1830 hours with a bomb-load of eighteen 1000-pound bombs plus incendiaries.

Over the enemy coast 'slight anti-aircraft fire' was encountered.

'We flew at 22 000 to 23 000 feet, he said, 'the night being clear with low temperatures. When we were about thirty minutes from the target a Pathfinder Force aircraft was shot down to the port of track. Due to the exploding of its target indicators and markers on the ground, many aircraft in the Main Force stream bombed these markers thus splitting up the compactness of the stream. At this stage, night fighters attacked us. After the first attack all our guns became unserviceable. Due to the freezing temperatures the breech-blocks of the guns had frozen in the forward position. We were an experienced crew and did not bomb the wrong PFF markers but carried on to the main target. Four more times we were attacked by fighters. Each time we took evasive action, only suffering a few bullet holes in the second and third attacks.'

For Pilot Officer John Goldsmith, a Canadian navigator with No. 625 Squadron, Kelstern, in No. 1 Group, the briefing was bad news. A Nova Scotian from Halifax, Goldsmith had been a student before joining the RCAF.

When the target was announced as Nuremberg he and his crew, he frankly recalls, were 'a little shaken up' because this would be the deepest penetration they had so far made into Germany. During that month of March, they had already flown on six major operations over Germany in their Lancaster III, CF-S, Serial Number ND 407—Stuttgart on 1 March when 4 aircraft were lost; Stuttgart again on 15 March, with 40 aircraft lost; Frankfurt, on 18 March with 22 aircraft lost; Frankfurt, again, on 22 March, with 33 aircraft lost; Berlin on 24 March with 73 aircraft lost; and Essen on 26 March with 9 aircraft lost.

As the navigator on all these operations Goldsmith's main reaction to the deep-penetration Nuremberg briefing was a feeling of tiredness and nervousness. Coincidentally, it was the crew's thirteenth operation.

Take-off was routine, if not exactly light-hearted, and Lancaster CF-S crossed the enemy coast heading south, on time as briefed. Checking, Goldsmith calculated that they must have turned east too early at Position *B* near Charleroi, for as they headed out on the long leg towards Nuremberg he confirmed that the aircraft was about ten miles north of track.

'There was plenty of fighter activity south of us,' Goldsmith recalls, 'so we stayed north of track until we turned onto our target run-in. The moon made it almost as light as day and the vapour trails of our bombers were very conspicuous. In the light of the moon it looked like a four-lane highway. We saw much air-to-air firing and sighted two enemy fighters and one of them nearly crashed into us, head-on, during the bombing run.'

Flying Officer S. H. Johnson, a navigator-set operator, with No. 156 Squadron, Warboys, a No. 8 (Pathfinder) Group squadron, noted only the customary crew reaction to the Nuremberg briefing when, as usual, the Lancaster's mid-upper gunner Arthur Irwin, from Birmingham, shook his head at the night sky and said glumly to Billie Love, the Australian rear-gunner, 'There's blood on the moon tonight, Bill.' With this lugubrious statement the tough, hard-bitten little Australian agreed. Then, again as usual, the mid-upper gunner from Birmingham began eating the flying rations he was supposed to keep for the return flight from the target.

Love, better known as the 'Dook of Sydney', was not only the incumbent of the rear turret of the crew's Lancaster X-XRAY but also virtually their mascot, and a popular squadron character.

Johnson recalls that he was short, square-shouldered, plain-spoken and aggressive. He was also intensely loyal and a natural imitator and comic and was regarded as 'terrific' by the English airmen whom he lampooned and entertained. To anybody approximating his own stature his invariable greeting was: 'The trouble with all you little blokes is that you have the same aggressive inferiority complex.' Squadron legend had it that on one memorable night the intercom warning he gave his pilot when the Lancaster was about to be attacked by a night fighter was the statement 'Love's last word is spoken—*dive port!*' Painted around his four-gun rear turret was the declaration 'Love will find a way'.

Despite his ebullient, if not irreverent, attitude towards the sombre business of night bombing, Love wore the ribbons of both the DFC and the DFM.

Flying with Johnson, the gloomy Arthur Irwin and the irrepressible William Johnson Harrigan Love were the English pilot, Squadron Leader Dickie Walbourn, DSO, DFC; the navigator-plotter, Squadron Leader Les Glasspool, RAF (later to die over Friedrichshaven); the English flight engineer, Sergeant Truman, and an RAF wireless air gunner, Wally Walker, DFC, from Sydney, Australia.

Johnson, a barrister and solicitor prior to enlistment with the RAAF, kept a dairy. The entry for the events of the night of 30 March 1944, was cryptic but to the point. After summing up the Nuremberg operation as a lengthy, tough grind, he commented: 'It was a hell of a long way into Germany and seemed as if it would never end. It was clear all the way into the target—too much moonlight and the Jerry fighters (which are licked, according to the papers) had a hey-day.'

Coming from a member of an experienced and well-knit Pathfinder crew the comment could be regarded as valid.

Stationed at RAF Ludford Magna in the Lincolnshire Wolds was No. 101 Squadron, a crack special-duties squadron in No. 1 Group, carrying out secret 'Airborne Cigar' operations. For one of the squadron's Lancaster pilots in 'A' Flight, Pilot Officer Robert McHattie, a Scot from Banffshire and a policeman prior to enlistment in the RAF, there was nothing in the Nuremberg briefing which seemed to indicate that this operation, his fourth, would be any different from the others. There was just one significant point—the fuel load. The squadron's Lancasters had been fuelled to the full capacity of their tanks—2154 gallons—so it was no surprise to McHattie when briefing revealed a red route-tape stretching deep into Germany to Nuremberg.

Like all Lancasters of Bomber Command's 'Airborne Cigar' special-duties squadrons, McHattie's would be carrying a crew of eight, not seven, to the target that night. Six of McHattie's crew were British by birth—Flight Sergeant Steven Wall, navigator; Flying Officer John Sutherland, bomb aimer; Flight Sergeant John Maxwell, flight engineer and a fellow Scot; Sergeant John Allison, wireless air gunner; Sergeant Colin Bleach, mid-upper gunner and Sergeant Kenneth Exelby, rear gunner.

The eighth member of the crew was British by naturalization—the special operator Sergeant Montague Barss. He also spoke German, a prerequisite for his skilled and lonely task. As usual, Barss would see nothing of the Nuremberg operation that night but the eerie flicker of electronic blips on a three-inch cathode ray cube, an integral part of the radar device code-named Airborne Cigar.

Isolated deep in the dark tunnel-like fuselage of the Lancaster with only the flying-booted feet of the mid-upper gunner, nearby for company, Barss would monitor the range of VHF voice radio transmissions between the German night-fighter controllers and their fighters. When an R/T transmission was seen as a blip on his screen, Barss would tune in on its frequency. Alone and in the dark, he would listen to the voice of the enemy. Once the signal was identified as a German transmission he would turn on one of three jamming transmitters and tune it to the Luftwaffe frequency. Jammed off the air the German controller would return on other frequencies but each time Barss would patiently hunt down the transmissions until he jammed these, too. For Barss and his fellow special operators of the Airborne Cigar squadrons this nightly game of electronic cat-and-mouse was as demanding as it was frustrating, if not disastrous, for the Luftwaffe controllers and their impatient pilots.

For its specialized role in the Nuremberg operation, No. 101 Squadron would as usual be flying its Lancasters spaced out at intervals of one minute along the bomber stream.

Climbing into flying gear, collecting flight rations and stowing escape kits in their battledress jacket pockets, McHattie and his crew were out at their waiting aircraft, a Lancaster Mark III, Serial No. DV 298 and squadron-coded SR-E, an hour before take-off. After checking all their equipment for serviceability they spent the last, long half-hour chatting with their ground crew and the crews of Lancasters at neighbouring dispersal points.

'It was a very cold, frosty evening,' McHattie recalls, 'and there was a cloudless sky with a very bright moon already high in the sky. A friendly aircraft passed overhead and, on looking up, I could see the aircraft's contrail clearly in the moonlight although I could not see the aircraft. This was a bad sign to me because I estimated the height of the contrail at about 15 000 feet and I turned to my crew and said that this indicated a record 'chop'. (The prophecy unfortunately proved correct, not as a percentage but in total aircraft lost on one raid.)

'Taxiing out and take-off were normal and we climbed to

6000 feet over base before setting course for rendezvous with the bomber stream at the enemy coast at the appointed time. I was detailed to a position near the front of the stream. Soon our troubles started. During initial climb the navigation lights refused to go out when switched off. This was easily remedied by removing the fuses. Before we reached the enemy coast the mid-upper gunner reported electrical failure. This would mean that he would have no suit-heating. It was a bitterly cold night: −45° centigrade at 21 000 feet and I felt sure he could not survive long as a useful crew member in these conditions. I ordered him to stay in his turret as long as he could but to vacate it before he lost consciousness and to go to the astro position and keep a fighter watch from there. About half an hour later he reported he was leaving his turret. By this time we were above 16 000 feet and making contrails. Enemy activity in the form of night fighters had begun and contrailing was consequently very dangerous. The enemy fighters merely had to fly along the contrails until they came to their quarry and then shoot it down.

'Enemy fighter activity increased until it reached its highest intensity at the Rhine. Numerous combats broke out on both sides and to our rear. Tracer criss-crossed the sky as fighter attacked and bomber replied. The path of the bomber stream, on the ground, was strewn with the burning wrecks of crashed bombers. A rocket-firing Junkers Ju 88 attacked us from extreme range but evasive action enabled me to watch the salvo go streaking harmlessly past us. Far away to port I could see a number of aircraft, away off track, coned in searchlights. It was probably Mainz. I saw one shot down. Some fifty miles from target a Lancaster corkscrewed downwards past my nose closely pursued by a Messerschmitt Me 110. Neither aircraft opened fire although the range was close. The intensive fighter activity seemed to have diminished as we approached the target'.

Flying with McHattie, wireless operator Sergeant John Allison also noted that it was bitterly cold when SR-E reached operational height. Even in Allison's radio position which was one of the warmest crew stations in the Lancaster, the cold was almost unbearable.

'As soon as we got over German territory it was clear that

it was going to be a big night. Swarms of enemy fighters took full advantage of the bright moonlight and all the way into the target . . . tracer from air combats streaked the sky around us. We strained our eyes in the darkness, expecting attack at any moment.

'. . . about half way to the target, a rocket tore towards us and Ken in the rear turret gave Mac, the skipper, directions for evasive action and we avoided it successfully. These rocket missiles looked like big balls of light leaving a trail of sparks behind them. They travelled fairly fast but it was usually possible to dodge them. Sometimes they seemed to follow you even if you took evasive action—rather shaking!

'Soon afterwards, Junior's mid-upper turret electrics packed up and with it his electric heating. Without this he was practically comatose in the intense cold so the skipper ordered him to keep watch from the astrodome beside me where he could have the benefit of the cabin heating.'

Clearly, according to this extract from the diary which Allison kept at the time, it was certainly a night to be remembered.

Another No. 101 Squadron pilot, Flight Lieutenant Robin Knights, DFC, RAF, captain of a crew in 'B' Flight, had not thought there was anything especially significant about the briefing at Ludford Magna. It was a routine briefing insofar as any operational briefing in Bomber Command could be described as 'routine', but there was, as Knights recalls it, the usual 'sinking feeling' when the target location was revealed as being so deep inside enemy territory.

Not that Knights and his crew of Englishmen lacked experience over Germany. Quite soon, in fact, their worth as an operational crew was to be recognized as follows: to Knights, a bar to his DFC and subsequent award of the DSO; to his navigator, Sergeant Pinner, to his flight engineer, Sergeant Ferry, and to his wireless air gunner, Sergeant Bromeley, the DFM, awarded on 12 November 1944; to his bomb aimer, Sergeant Morgan, commissioned in June 1944, the DFC, also awarded on 12 November 1944; and to his rear gunner, Sergeant Murphy, commissioned in April 1944, the DFC, on 20 October 1944.

Morgan and the mid-upper gunner, Sergeant Hart, were second-tour veterans who had replaced Knights' original two gunners, killed over Berlin on 20 January 1944. Wounded on the same night had been their eighth crew member, another German-speaking special operator of the Airborne Cigar monitoring and jamming equipment, Flying Officer Feurgeson Smith, DFC and bar. After Berlin his place in the crew was taken by Flying Officer Crosette. (Smith subsequently became a detective chief inspector with Scotland Yard's Special Branch.)

Robin Knights had been a farm worker and a regular soldier before transferring to the RAF in June 1941.

Such, then, was the 'gen' crew which was to set out on what appeared to be yet another routine, if lengthy, attack on a German target.

Knights' Lancaster, Serial No. LL 773 and squadron-coded SR-D, was carrying, in addition to the maximum fuel load of 2154 gallons, a 'cookie'—a 4000-pound high-blast 'blockbuster' bomb—and fourteen containers of clustered thermite incendiary bombs for fire-raising.

The main impression that Knights retains of the events after take-off is of 'a long drag on a very dark night'.

He recalls seeing a few flares of the type then believed to be dropped by the German night fighters along the route of the bomber stream but he did not see any of the flares customarily dropped by RAF Pathfinder aircraft to mark navigational turning-points for the main force.

'There was a feeling that forecast winds were wrong,' he said, 'and that navigation was awry. Turns on track were made on DR (dead reckoning) and at the elapsed ETA for the target nothing was seen of PFF flares or of fires. In the current slang we 'stooged around a bit'. This was when we began to see other aircraft, mostly going in the opposite direction. This, I think, was where the night fighters began to take effect as we began to see combats taking place. After a short while a fire was seen to be started some way off and the place had a cone of searchlights over it. This, we thought, might be Nuremberg and I headed towards it. So did a few hundred other Lancasters and there were some good fires going by the time we began a run-up.'

For Sergeant George Dykes, a Scots-born Canadian rear gunner from Saskatoon, Saskatchewan, in 'B' Flight of No. 433 Squadron, based at Skipton-on-Swale, in No. 6 Group, the Nuremberg briefing had been remarkable only for the fact that the met. officer had been 'a bit vague' about what the weather would be like over the target.

Dykes' crew consisted of another Canadian, Sergeant Douglas Carruthers, mid-upper gunner; four Englishmen— Pilot Officer Ronald Reinelt, pilot; Sergeant John Hardes, navigator; Pilot Officer George Wade, bomb aimer, Sergeant J. Peppercorn, flight engineer—and a lone Welsh wireless air gunner whom George regretfully remembers only as 'Taffy'.

Take-off for the crew, in their Halifax Mark III Q-QUEEN, was at 2145 and was without incident. George does remember discussions between the pilot and the flight engineer about the sluggish performance of the Halifax and that climbing to the prescribed height of 20 000 feet before crossing the Dutch coast was not easily achieved.

'Flak was light along our track on the way in,' George said, 'and we did not see any enemy aircraft. As a matter of fact we did not see too many of our own aircraft despite the fact that there were about 800 bombers taking part.'

Such were the curious inconsistencies of fact generally associated with furtive forays carried out under cover of darkness by Bomber Command.

Over the target area at Nuremberg, however, there was to be no shortage of action for the Canadian rear gunner and his crew.

At Breighton, in No. 4 Group, a No. 78 Squadron Scots flight engineer from Inverness and former taxi driver, Sergeant David Davidson, was facing his crew's second operational flight. As a new crew in the Halifax squadron they still did not have their own aircraft. The one allocated to them on this day was an old stand-by aircraft, but still a Halifax Mark III such as the rest of the squadron would be flying.

By 1030 Davidson, as flight engineer, was out at the dispersals checking over Halifax EY-A and cleaning the perspex panels of the cockpit. The ground crew succeeded in convincing him that although EY-A was old she had no 'snags'.

It was then that Davidson noticed that the ground staff were fitting overload fuel tanks in the belly of the aircraft and immediately there was much joking about the prospects of spending the night over Berlin.

By 1500, bombing-up had begun at Breighton with tractors and low-slung bomb trolleys rolling around the perimeter track to the dispersals where the empty bomb-bays were waiting. Davidson cycled back out to EY-A to see what kind of a bomb-load was being winched up to the racks. Now his crew believed him: the bomb-load was incendiaries only so that an overload fuel tank could be fitted in the belly compartment. There was no doubt now that it was going to be a long trip.

With Davidson that night would be his pilot, Flight Sergeant P. E. Christiansen, RCAF; the navigator, Sergeant King, RAF; the bomb aimer, Sergeant J. Liston, RCAF; the wireless operator, Sergeant A. Hale, RAF; the mid-upper gunner, Sergeant H. Darani, RAF; and the rear gunner, Sergeant A. Fleet, RCAF. They were the newest crew in 'B' Flight.

At 1930 Davidson sat down to flying supper with his crew. There was not much talk in the mess that evening but everybody, Davidson recalled later, looked washed, shaved and very neat. 'There was an atmosphere like you get before a big show begins,' he recollected.

Briefing for No. 78 Squadron was at 2030. The scene was a familiar one but Davidson still remembers it: 'Dozens of crews can be seen cycling from the perimeter track towards the briefing hut. Inside now. The wall map stands out as we enter. All eyes follow the route ribbon. Long, very long, it is. As we get near the front our navigator mumbles "Nuremberg". Groans are heard from crews entering and seeing the route.'

For the rest of the briefing Davidson was preoccupied with his own worries, as flight engineer, about fuel tank drills and engine-handling techniques for conservation of fuel. The Nuremberg trip, he sensed, would mean that he would have to watch over every drop of petrol in EY-A's tanks.

The subsequent events of that night are best described in Davidson's own narrative, a simple but vivid document with a wealth of attention to time and detail:

'2115: Briefing over, everybody walking down to parachute section to collect gear. Hanging about now, smoking and nattering and waiting for the crew buses to arrive. I get into conversation with rear gunner of z-zebra. This is his first trip. His captain is Sergeant Hampson. They have just come off leave. We exchange take-off times. They are taking off two minutes ahead of us. "See you later," I said but it was to be two years later at Catterick camp before I was to see him again.

'The crew buses arrive. There are three crews in ours: Sergeant Hampson for z-zebra; an Australian—Constable, I think his name was, and his crew for h-howe and ourselves for a-able. Hampson and his crew get out first. Then it's our turn. As the bus pulls away I walk towards the Halifax. My God, it looks so large in the dark. A good-luck round and then everybody's aboard. The ground staff corporal gets the pilot to sign the Form 700. He wishes me good luck on the way out. I go down the fuselage with him to check "Door shut" at 2150.

'2152: Start-up. 2159: Chocks away. Moving out of dispersal and waving to ground crew. Join the queue for the runway with our brakes squealing as we slew round to catch some wind in the engine cowlings to keep our cylinder-head temperatures down. A green from the ACP to turn onto the runway. 2209: Throttles opening up power with brakes on. Brakes off and we are away. We are swinging. Straight again, on and on with the nose down. Then we lift and climb away slowly. 2210: Time to set course. We keep climbing on course at 2400 rmp and +2 boost but this kite is slow.

'2300: Out over the English Channel now. The French coast is coming up. It looks big and dark against the sea. 2325: We cross north of Cape Gris Nez. 2326: Rear gunner reports flak off port quarter but quite some distance away. 2334: Fighter flares are dropped close to starboard. 2335: Combat reported to starboard and below us. There is a Halifax on fire. We can see the square fins. 2336: The fire in the other Halifax goes out. There is no explosion. 2338: Three combats are reported to port and ahead of us. 2340: Two explosions are seen on the ground ahead of us and to starboard of track. Quite a lot is going on and so soon. We are still climbing on course. The moon has come up. It shook us a bit because it came out of the cloud looking like a Jerry fighter flare and both our gunners started firing at it. When we realized it was really the moon it was a relief to be able to laugh. We are now making vapour trails. Quite a few of our kites are above us and in front of us but not many behind.

'0045: King, the navigator, reports to the skipper that we are ten minutes late and suggests we return to base as we will be too late to bomb with the main stream. Christiansen says, "No, we go. We're too far in now to start arsing about." The crew agrees. The navigator says "OK. I told you." '

At 0018, Davidson could see the target coming up.

For Pilot Officer Raymond Curling, an Australian Lancaster pilot in 'A' Flight, No. 622 Squadron, Mildenhall, in No. 3 Group, Nuremberg would be his sixth operation.

His crew was a typical Bomber Command amalgam— navigator: Flight Sergeant Featherstonehaugh, RNZAF; bomb aimer: Flight Sergeant Short, RNZAF; flight engineer: Sergeant Humphrier, RAF; wireless air gunner: flight Sergeant Smith, RAAF; mid-upper gunner: Sergeant Harris, RAF; rear gunner: Sergeant Russell, RAF. The five trips they had already flown together had not been uneventful. In 42.30 operational hours they had experienced flak damage, fighter attack and a mid-air collision.

Referring to his war-time diary, Ray Curling recalls:

'On this occasion, "Butch" Harris decided to take a risk on the moon which was almost full and ideal for enemy fighters. By 10.00 p.m. we were well on the way. As soon as we reached the enemy coast the enemy defences went in to attack. We were equipped with an instrument called "Boozer". This was a warning device in the form of two lights in the pilot's cockpit. One, a yellow light, would blink on if an enemy aircraft picked the aircraft up on his radar beam and the other light, a red one, would warn of anti-aircraft ground defences. In the event of either coming on we would immediately go into evasive action. The instrument had a reputation of going haywire.

'As soon as we reached enemy territory I thought my Boozer had gone berserk but the convincing puffs of black smoke behind us confirmed that the ack-ack indicator was working OK. From that point to the target, enemy fighters seemed to be on us in swarms and the sky was continually criss-crossed with tracers. It was truly grim and we were extremely tensed. Every second I was waiting for the word from my gunners to weave. We were not attacked. All we could see was my little light blinking from time to time, streams of tracer and the all-too-frequent sight of a dead aircraft diving to earth in flames.'

By the time Curling reached the target at 0125 he estimated that he had about six- to seven-tenths of cloud cover at 20 000 feet.

The early disappearance of cloud cover concerned Flight Sergeant R. W. Parissien, a wireless air gunner with a Pathfinder squadron, No. 156, based at RAF Station, Upwood. They were an all-English crew—pilot, Warrant Officer Higgs; navigator, Flying Officer D. J. Chase; bomb aimer, Flight Sergeant Keating; flight engineer, Sergeant Webb; mid-upper gunner, Sergeant Woodhead and rear gunner, Sergeant Webb.

Parissien, formerly a clerk from Bromley, Kent, was anticipating the forecast eight- to nine-tenths cloud as his Lancaster GT-C climbed away from Upwood, carrying support and marker flares as well as incendiaries and high-explosive bombs.

'The usual flak was encountered en route,' he recalls, 'but what was more disturbing was the break-up of cloud revealing a bright moon. This naturally resulted in heavy flak and fighter activity throughout the length of the route over German territory towards the target.

'Before reaching our target it became clear that the whole of the main force were being subjected to intense fighter attack, assisted, of course, by ground-directed searchlights. I saw two aircraft going down in flames but could not identify them.'

Another Pathfinder airman, Flight Sergeant W. D. Ogilvie, of No. 635 Squadron, was destined never to reach Nuremberg. Near Koblenz, on the Rhine, his Lancaster was hit by flak fired from a battery to the north of the city. The target-indicater flare in the bomb-bay, intended to identify Nuremberg with characteristic brilliance, ignited and burned through the metal control rods to the elevators and rudders. Further aft, beyond the bomb-bay, the bomb-sized photographic flash flare exploded in searing white light, burning a large hole in the fuselage. Aglow with the lurid light of its own pyrotechnics, the Lancaster had itself become a target. Petrol was streaming from ruptured wing tanks when Ogilvie's pilot, J. Nicholls, ordered his crew to bale out. Apart from a cracked ankle, Ogilvie landed safely in Germany. Ahead of him was capture, interrogation and a series of camps ending at Luckenwalde, south of Berlin.

'I wish to forget it,' he said. 'The sooner we all forget it the better. It was a bloody business.'

Luckier that night was another airman from the same group —an Australian navigator, Flying Officer W. J. Barclay, from Melbourne, Victoria.

Barclay's crew was the typical Bomber Command mix— pilot, Pilot Officer W. J. Taggart, Australian; second navigator, Flight Lieutenant Nathan Crawford, Canadian; bomb aimer, Pilot Officer Wray Paterson, Canadian; flight engineer, Flight Sergeant Hart, English; wireless air gunner, Pilot Officer Alan Robb, Australian; mid-upper gunner, Flight Sergeant Derek Hughes, English; and rear gunner, Pilot Officer J. H. de Tores, an Australian from Lismore, New South Wales.

It was the crew's third Pathfinder Force operation after having transferred to No. 156 Squadron from No. 460 (RAAF) Squadron where they had flown nineteen trips.

Barclay's account of the events of that night was brief but business-like:

'2145: Boarded aircraft.

'2228. Took off. Climbed over base and set course 2239.

'2314.6: Reached *A*, first turning point, after dog-legging to lose three minutes on this leg. (Crossed enemy coast 2327.8.) The second leg took us over Ghent and to the southwest of Brussels on which we fixed position by radar (H2S).

'2348.1: Arrived *B*, set course for *C*. This leg took us

between Bonn and Koblenz. At 0003.5 passed red navigation flare dropped just south of Aachen.

'0007: Sighted green target-indicators of dummy raid being made on Koln.

'0048.3: Arrived *C*, set course for target.'

At Leeming, in Yorkshire, a Buckinghamshire-born RAF flight engineer, Flight Sergeant L. A. Pratt, was the only Englishman in the crew of a Halifax Mark III, v-VICTOR, in 'B' Flight of No. 427 (RCAF) Squadron.

Apart from the navigator Dick Morrison, who was USAF, the rest of the crew were all Canadians—pilot, Rex Clibbery, DFM; bomb aimer, Norman Nash, DFC; wireless air gunner, Jimmy Jardine; mid-upper gunner, Dick Qualle; rear gunner Billy 'Shorty' Martin.

'I remember Nuremberg very well,' Pratt recalls. 'Particularly so, perhaps, because within my crew I was regarded as having a good pair of night eyes and was continuously pressured to keep my head in the astrodome and look out. This was because we were a jumpy crew having experienced several fighter attacks, one in particular with quite disastrous but, for us, lucky results.

'This night on Nuremberg was also memorable because we lost both of the squadron's flight commanders—Squadron Leader Laird and Squadron Leader Bisset. Laird must have been on almost the last trip of his second tour and Bisset was a second tour man. I remember too, that Harry Glass, a flight engineer with No. 429 (Bison) Squadron, RCAF, also at Leeming, got the CGM for conduct after being shot up and having to ditch.

'Briefing, to the best of my knowledge, was in the late afternoon or early evening. I don't remember too much about it except that we were carrying an overload fuel tank and this I had already established in the morning visit to the aircraft.

'The met. man told us it would be bright moonlight with little or no cloud cover and a long straight leg in from the enemy coast to the target and a particularly long swoop outgoing to low-level over Vichy, France. The reason for the trip was given as a conference or meeting of top. Nazis including Hitler at Nuremberg at that time. We had the additional job of sending winds. Our load was, I think, nine cans of incendiaries and a 4000-pounder.

'I can remember discussing the pros and cons with our pilot, Rex Clibbery, just after marshalling the aircraft. In fact, Rex was leaning against the starboard wheel at the time. I expressed my doubts about the trip in no uncertain manner but he was quite adamant that it would be scrubbed like a few others had at about that time. Looking back, I feel that this was a bit of bravado and perhaps a little wishful thinking on his part. I had the feeling, as I'm sure the rest of the crew did, that this one wasn't going to be easy, a little different to some of the ops on buzz-bomb sites and railway marshalling yards which had been done quite frequently at about that time.'

Pratt's main recollection of the take-off in their Halifax v-VICTOR was rueful recognition of the fact that they did not get, as his pilot had claimed they would, the 'ops scrubbed' flare from the control tower. Airborne at 1908, the flight to the enemy coast was uneventful.

'After crossing and now being at 20 000 feet we were amazed at the terrific range of visibility in the full moonlight,' said Pratt. 'One could see many of the aircraft in the stream. As the met. man had said, there was no cloud cover.

'Near Cologne, Clibbery suddenly put the nose of the aircraft very sharply down into a dive. He shouted "Didn't anybody see that boy?" and a Fw 190 went from nose to tail over the top of us and carried straight on. We were then fully alert. I knew I was going to turn in another lousy log as my head had to be in the astrodome from now on. Norman Nash, at his H2S set, was bawled at to get his head down in the nose (watching for fighters) and to stop "playing navigators". Aft of my station at the astrodome, Qualle's mid-upper turret was whizzing around to beat all hell.

'We had the sky pretty well divided up—Clibbery, the pilot, looked dead ahead; Nash, the navigator, looked underneath from the nose; "Shorty" Martin, the rear gunner, scanned the rear upper and low quarters; Qualle, in the mid-upper, watched both sides; I took the two forward upper quarters; Jimmy Jardine, the wireless op, covered underneath with "Fishpond".*

'We saw tracer exchanged behind us and saw some aircraft catch fire. Then there was tracer ahead and on the port side. Aircraft started to burn and go down. A few miles on we saw aircraft burning on the ground, quite a few of them in fact. Someone said, "Look at all those damn Jerry scarecrows". Again this was wishful thinking. We decided to weave a bit and did the occasional corkscrew. This we did from time to time, right through to the target, particularly when things got quiet and we got that sort of feeling. We saw quite a few jettisoned loads of incendiaries. There were some fighter flares about—not too many, though—but I actually saw a Ju 88 drop right above us. It seemed almost as though it just missed and nearly hit our wing. More corkscrews. Between us we called several evasive tactics as we saw aircraft coming in close. I remember calling a couple myself nearer to the target area when things had darkened up a bit. We still saw what appeared to be aircraft burning on the deck.'

For an Australian pilot, Pilot Officer E. A. Mustard, of No. 463 (Australian) Squadron, at Waddington, Nuremberg was to prove to be what he later described as 'A long, deadly haul through a reception committee'.

Nuremberg would be his seventh trip over Germany, including two as a second pilot on joining the squadron's 'A' Flight, and the fifth with his current crew: Flight Sergeant W. H. Goodwin, RAF, navigator; Flight Sergeant A. P. Mustard, RCAF, bomb aimer; Sergeant S. B. Maltman, RAF, flight engineer; Sergeant H. McClelland, RAF, wireless air gunner; Sergeant D. A. L. Herbert, RAF, mid-upper gunner; Flight Sergeant T. K. Wills, RAAF, rear gunner.

Pilot Officer Mustard lifted his Lancaster, C-CHARLIE, off the runway at Waddington at 2215 and not without relief was he safely airborne.

'A word about the kite,' he said. 'She was an old veteran from a Lancaster finishing school with thousands of circuits

---

* 'Fishpond' was a radar device which warned of the proximity and approach of enemy fighters and was also valuable as a collision-avoidance aid in the bomber stream.

and bumps to her credit. Serial No. L 7539. Engines were Merlins Mark XX with no boost over-ride for take-off. This reduced the all-up weight for take-off by about one ton and while it wasn't very satisfying to hear the reduced bomb-load being read out at briefing it was very useful to be able to bomb from the top of the stack and still have no petrol worries on the way home.

'Memories of the trip centre around the leg from *B* to *C*, from approximately fifteen miles north-east of Charleroi to approximately 50° 30′ North, 10° 40′ East. This was a leg of about 160 miles and was considered by all to be too far to fly in a straight line over enemy territory. Was it ever! There was also a feeling that so-called navigation aids in the form of TIs dropped along the track were liable to "bring the flies". This device was used south of Aachen.

'At this period, the Germans were using various types of so-called scarecrows in the form of pyrotechnics to intimidate our crews and, in fact, the gunners would often argue "Kite or scarecrow?" when reporting lights in the air or on the ground. I do remember that on this night our navigator told the gunners: "Shut up. I'm too busy to log all that stuff." There clearly was a lot of activity and it seemed unbelievable that each fire in the sky was another of our kites going down. After logging some air-to-air combats and flamers going down, the navigator finally gave it up.'

For Flight Lieutenant Burrows, of No. 44 Squadron, the trip out over the English coast and the North Sea from Dunholme Lodge was without incident. Being heavily laden with maximum fuel as well as the bombs, the Lancaster climbed slowly to an operational height of about 18 000 feet. Weather conditions improved gradually and on crossing the enemy coast there was good visibility with patchy cloud. The navigator, Stancer, reported tersely that the forecast winds were 'a lot of bull'.

'With a heavy tail-wind our ground speed was so good that we had to dog-leg to enable us to be at our turning-points promptly and so stay with the Main Force,' said Burrows. Over the enemy coast the rear gunner, Hall, reported another aircraft closing from starboard, too close for comfort.

A Lancaster or a Halifax, also dog-legging to lose time so as to stay with the flight-plan, slid over the top of Burrows' Lancaster, missing it by about twenty-five feet.

'The incident passed and everything appeared to be quiet again,' said Burrows. 'However, after travelling approximately twenty miles inland things really began to happen. There appeared to be combats going on all around us with the consequent explosions of raiding aircraft receiving direct hits. Some blew up so close to us that the whole of our aircraft shuddered alarmingly, as if every rivet would pop out of its socket.

'It was our duty to report each combat to the navigator who logged same, viz. height, time, speed, position, etc. After approximately ten aircraft had thus been reported the skipper told the crew to disregard this order. The atmosphere was rather tense. I however continued to do so and was frightened out of my wits when he (the skipper) dug me in the ribs and shouted "I said enough!" '

Under conditions which seemed ideal for the defences, with little or no cloud protection, it seemed to Burrows that the way in to the target seemed to last for 'ages' with the British force obviously suffering alarming casualties.

Near Frankfurt, Burrows' Lancaster was coned and held by searchlights for 'some considerable time' with the pilot, Wing Commander Thompson, taking violent evasive action. During this time the crew noticed that no flak came up, thus indicating that German fighters were operating in the area.

'Our first combat happened after approximately one hour but, most fortunately, the rear gunner saw this Fw 190 trying to get into position and directed us clear, losing him fairly easily. This was most remarkable as the conditions were ideal. This happened two or three times. We saw fighters going towards other aircraft and exchanging shots but were left alone most of the time ourselves. The final number of attackers sighted, going towards the target, were too numerous to mention.'

There were no qualms about going to Nuremberg for Sergeant Ted Shaw, a Canadian rear gunner in a Lancaster crew of 'B' Flight, No. 12 Squadron, Wickenby, Lincolnshire, in No. 5 Group.

A stockbrokers' salesman from Moncton, New Brunswick, Shaw had attended briefing cheerfully enough with his crew: Pilot Officer A. W. Moore, pilot, from Berkshire; Warrant Officer J. T. Goodrick, navigator, an Australian; Flight Sergeant P. Hocking, wireless air gunner, a Devon man; Flight Sergeant R. Robinson, bomb aimer, a Welshman from Colwyn Bay; Flight Sergeant P. Peters, mid-upper gunner from Doncaster in Yorkshire; Flight Sergeant T. Ferguson, flight engineer, another Welshman.

The reason for Sergeant Shaw's prematurely relaxed approach was that the strategy of the attack as explained at briefing was that there would be several diversionary raids and this would appear to be another attack on Berlin.

'It was felt that fighter opposition would be concentrated around Berlin and that this could be a rather easy trip,' he recalls. The crew's optimism was destined to be short-lived.

'I think that the most memorable part of the briefing was the met. officer's forecast of five- to seven-tenths cloud which proved to be completely wrong,' he said. 'After we had crossed the enemy coast it was a brilliant moonlit night with practically no cloud. It was so clear that we could easily make out other aircraft in the bomber stream.

'According to my log book, take-off was at 2159 hours. The bomb-load consisted of a 4000-pound blockbuster and incendiaries. On crossing the Channel, I watched the explosion of the bomb load of an aborted aircraft from about 7000 feet. I had never seen a big one blow up so close and was amazed at the power and the pink and orange fire which seemed to last for about twenty or thirty seconds.

'Upon reaching the enemy coast the usual flak and lights were encountered but we had no trouble until we were approaching the target.

'For the first time on our tour we sighted flaming objects, resembling burning aircraft, floating in the sky and which, I believe, were called scarecrows.

'Night-fighter opposition became very heavy about thirty minutes from the target and numerous attacks on our aircraft were sighted. One I remember in particular: a Lancaster flying straight and level was being attacked time and again. Apparently those on board were either dead or wounded because there was no evasive action being taken and no opposition from the gunners. The moonlight and the reflected light from the snow on the ground made it almost like twilight.

'A few minutes later we were attacked by a Focke Wulf Fw 190 which made a pass at us from slightly below port. I called to the skipper to turn hard to port just before he opened fire and he missed us. By this time we were perhaps six or seven minutes away from the target which was burning very well.

'All of a sudden there was a tremendous pounding and vibration. Another fighter had attacked us from below and we had flown through its fire. Both the mid-upper and I hose-piped it as it turned away and it appeared to have been hit. This attack caused considerable damage to the aircraft and started a fire in the bomb-bay. One of the blades of the starboard inner engine was holed and bent causing the skipper considerable trouble in controlling the aircraft.

'The third attack happened about a minute later. All I remember of this attack was glimpsing the tracer coming at me. One of the shells hit the gun stanchion in front of me and exploded. The explosion blinded me, blackening both my eyes and some of the fragments entered my left eye. This attack cut off the intercom, oxygen and hydraulic systems to my rear turret. The aircraft was taking violent evasive action and I did not know whether or not it was out of control.'

Meanwhile another Lancaster crew from Lincolnshire, skippered by Warrant Officer R. W. D. Price, a Canadian from Lloydminster, Saskatchewan, was enjoying the uneventful kind of night that Shaw had innocently been anticipating.

Price, a pilot in 'B' Flight of No. 625 Squadron, RAF Kelstern, was flying D-DOG, a Lancaster Mark III, Serial No. ND 619.

'All that I can recall is that there seemed to be much more enemy night-fighter activity than usual and quite heavy anti-aircraft fire,' he said. 'On this particular trip we were lucky as we sustained no damage to the aircraft and no injuries to the crew'.

Price's crew consisted of two Australians—Pilot Officer Dudley Ball, navigator, and Sergeant Jack Conley, bomb aimer—and four Englishmen—Sergeant Les Knowles, flight engineer; Sergeant Jim Harris, wireless air gunner; Sergeant Harry Powter, mid-upper gunner and Sergeant Frank Sutton, rear gunner.

Price had only 'a very hazy recollection' that there were more casualties than usual on the Nuremberg operation.

Unlike the Canadian pilot, Price, Flight Sergeant W. A. Stenning, a Surrey-born wireless air gunner in 'B' Flight, of No. 51 Squadron at Snaith, Yorkshire, in No. 4 Group, was to retain anything but hazy memories of the way into Nuremberg. For William Albert Stenning, a former motor-cycle salesman, this was his first operation and he was not likely to forget it. Nor were his crew mates who, except for the American pilot, Flight Lieutenant J. Pawell, were all British: Flight Sergeant R. F. Clark, navigator; Flight Sergeant R. Burgett, bomb aimer; Flight Sergeant A. Barnard, flight engineer; Sergeant W. Matthews, mid-upper gunner; Sergeant J. Baxter, rear gunner, and a Scot.

Stenning and his crew had arrived at RAF Station, Snaith, on 27 March from forty-eight hours leave after having completed a conversion course from Whitleys to Halifaxes at No. 1652 Heavy Conversion Unit, Marston Moor, where the previous commanding officer, Group Captain Cheshire, VC, had left his mark regarding crew discipline, both in the air and on the ground.

With 'Nobby' Clarke, the navigator, and Alf Barnard, the flight engineer, he reported to the Snaith guard-room on arrival from London and after signing in they were driven by a WAAF driver to their billet. It was a Nissen hut about a mile away, almost in the village of Pollington. The hut was deserted. Unknown to Stenning and his crew mates the other occupants had gone to Berlin that night.

'About four in the morning I heard them come in and remember listening to three of them discussing what must have been their worst-ever trip,' said Stenning. 'Apparently the squadron lost two crews that night.' It was a typical welcome to Bomber Command.

Shaken awake by a corporal next morning, Stenning was told to report to his pilot, Flight Lieutenant Pawell at 'B' Flight.

'We were straight away on a familiarization flight,' Stenning recalls. 'We were also detailed for ops that night but the squadron was stood down due to weather. Next day the weather was again dicey but we were given a five-hour cross country and then, hardly having had time to think much or look around, 30 March was with us and ops were on again and briefing scheduled for 1830 hours.

'This was our first ops briefing and I can still remember the armed SPs all standing guard at the briefing-room doors. About 150 of us were present and the big map board was covered. We know overload tanks had been fitted but this, at that stage, didn't mean much to me.

'Group Captain Fresson, DFC, entered and our squadron's commanding officer, Wing Commander Ling, opened the proceedings. I remember the cover coming off the briefing map and looking at this long, long red tape which seemed to stretch a hell of a long way into Germany. It must have also impressed the others judging by the remarks I overheard.

'The wing commander informed us that we would be that second wave of a heavy attack on Nuremberg and warned new crews, including us, about keeping in the Main Force bomber stream. Weather seemed good and apart from a long trip carrying mainly 500-pound HE bombs and incendiaries it all sounded fairly straightforward. We were to go out over the east coast and cross the enemy coast somewhere below the Frisian Islands.

'There was to be a feint attack on Berlin while we maintained a course to Nuremberg. Intelligence spoke of expected night-fighter opposition, flak areas on the way back and the fact that Nuremberg was a city with many old timbered buildings.

'There was a separate signals briefing which I attended and, as a newcomer, was duly detailed to go around the dispersals and check huge quantities of 'window' parcels for each of the aircraft.

'We met in the sergeants' mess for the ops meal at about

2000. Take-off was scheduled for 2130. By 2100 we were on the crew bus and soon out at the aircraft, checking and re-checking. Wilf Matthews, our mid-upper gunner, looked like a commando with his two knives, a Colt .45 and a police truncheon.

'During engine run-up the pilot and the flight engineer had some trouble on the port inner motor with some un-expected magneto drop which had not been there during the morning's run-up. The ground crew gave the all-clear after some minutes and all seemed OK on re-starting the motor.

'Up to twenty-eight aircraft were taking off that night from Snaith with us about half-way in the line-up. Back in the rest position we prepared for take-off as we saw the green from the ACP.

'Airborne, we circled base keeping a look out for aircraft coming up from Burn only a few miles away. I could see the lights at Selby and Goole and didn't think much of the black-out. We climbed to about 5000 feet and then set course for The Wash where we were to cross the coast.

'Joe Pawell, our American skipper (in the RCAF), was chewing his usual Phillies cigar which he never lit but always rolled around until it was oxygen time.

'We climbed to about 12 000 feet over the North Sea and after what seemed a short time the flight engineer kicked me on the shoulder to come and have a look from the astrodome. (In a Halifax the wireless air gunner's station was down in the nose-section, with the navigator and bomb aimer forward of the cockpit.) There were flares ahead and it looked like a never-ending line ahead with flares making a sort of avenue for us to fly down.

'Wilf Matthews, in the mid-upper turret, was giving us a running commentary and occasional warnings of other aircraft to port and starboard.

'I saw a huge burst in the sky ahead of us over the enemy coast and on the intercom someone said "They've had it" but it may have been a scarecrow fired up.

'I went back down into the nose and spoke to Bob Clarke, the navigator, who had been very quiet and matter-of-fact. He wasn't at all surprised that we were well and truly in the bomber stream.

'Out of my little port window I could see flak coming up. It seemed very light with all the flares around us. I was now studying Fishpond very closely and imagining all sorts of blips coming but they were probably interference at that stage. Soon there were reports from the flight engineer and the gunners of activity above and below. They hadn't seen any fighters yet but it was obvious that they were about. I saw a lot of flak ahead and to port followed by two very big explosions in the air. I could see an aircraft falling away in pieces. This was the first I had ever seen shot down but the feeling I had was that it just couldn't happen to us.

'We were heading towards the target on time with regular broadcasts coming in on W/T at fifteen minutes and forty-five minutes past the hour when a signal came through warning all aircraft to listen out on the "Tinsel" frequency. I tuned in and heard German controllers saying "Victor, Victor"* or something similar.

'As briefed, I banged away on the morse key, using the carbon mike in the engine nacelle. I could hear our operators in other aircraft sending out a sort of distorted message in morse. I picked up one—John, from Nottingham—and sent back—Bill, from Guildford—and we exchanged OK signals. I wondered if this really disturbed the German night-fighter frequencies.

'Soon after this I could hear the navigator telling the pilot to turn starboard towards the target. We were now at about 18 000 feet and I could see some fires on the ground, to port. Night-fighter activity was increasing with tracer appearing in the bomber stream. About 1.00 a.m. I went around with coffee for the crew and checked that the photoflash flare was OK and ready to go as we bombed.

'So far, it had been a fairly quiet night and I settled down and, as briefed, began dropping window.'

From the nose, the prone bomb aimer, Bob Burgett, reported sighting the target. The Halifax's radio was switched to Master Bomber frequency.

It would not be long now.

---

*'Victor' was the Luftwaffe's equivalent of the RAF and USAF's affirmative 'Roger'.

Flying in another No. 4 Group Halifax this night as a sergeant navigator, unaware that he had actually been commissioned since 21 March, just nine days earlier, was Pilot Officer J. L. Lambert in 'A' Flight, No. 578 Squadron, RAF Station, Burn.

This was to be Lambert's last flight with his crew: Pilot Officer C. J. Barton, pilot; Pilot Officer G. W. Crate, RCAF, bomb aimer; Sergeant M. E. Trousdale, flight engineer; Sergeant J. A. Kay, wireless air gunner; Sergeant H. Woods, mid-upper gunner; Sergeant F. Brice, rear gunner. They were all English except the bomb aimer, Crate.

No. 578 Squadron had been formed in January 1944 at RAF Station, Snaith. Lambert and his crew had been transferred from No. 78 Squadron at Breighton to form a nucleus as 'C' Flight of No. 51 Squadron to convert onto the new Halifax Mark III. The considerably improved performance and higher operational ceiling of the aircraft was greatly appreciated by the converting crews.

After a raid on Berlin on 30 January 1944, the new No. 578 Squadron moved from Snaith to Burn. The first operation flown from Burn was against Augsburg on 25 February.

March had been a particularly busy month with six major operations flown during the fourteen days culminating in the flight to Nuremberg on 30 March.

Take-off, in their Halifax LK-E, was at about 2200 hours. The crew's principal worry this night was the bright moonlight although, as usual, Lambert saw little from his navigation position of what was happening outside. Busy as he was with head down over his charts and log, Lambert was nevertheless concerned at the number of crew intercom reports about aircraft being shot down.

'We were equipped with tail-warning radar,' Lambert recalls, 'but this became unserviceable early in the night.'

This was soon to prove to be a lethal malfunction.

For a Canadian in another Halifax Mark III in the bomber stream that night—Pilot Officer A. L. Christner, a rear gunner with No. 429 Squadron, Leeming, Yorkshire, in No. 6 Group—the journey to Nuremberg was strangely uneventful.

'This was our fourth trip over Germany,' Christner recalls. 'I saw fires and explosions all the way to the target. In fact, I reported to our skipper, Flight Lieutenant A. I. MacDonald, a fellow Canadian, that everyone in the Main Force bomber stream was dropping their loads early but in reality what I had been seeing was our own bombers being shot down. Strangely, we didn't see a German fighter during the trip but then we'd already had our fun on the trip before with fighters at Frankfurt.'

Such was Christner's spare recollections of that night of fire.

For still another Canadian rear gunner in No. 6 Group, Pilot Officer J. G. McLauchlan, the Nuremberg operation had a special significance. It was the thirtieth and last that he would fly with his crew: Pilot Officer Chris Nielsen, pilot; Pilot Officer Don Awrey, navigator; Warrant Officer Les Milward, bomb aimer; Sergeant Chris Panten, flight engineer; Warrant Officer Harry Cooper, wireless air gunner; Sergeant John Patterson, mid-upper gunner.

On returning to the flare-path at RAF Station, Skipton Bridge, Yorkshire, that night, the crew would be saying goodbye to 'B' Flight and No. 433 Squadron. Screened from operations after surviving a full tour of thirty trips, they would be sent back to Canada as instructors. McLauchlan had already chosen the RCAF station in Canada where he would be posted. Yet, uneasily, he could not really believe that their luck would last.

Observing ground crews fitting overload fuel tanks to the Halifaxes, McLauchlan hoped that the long-distance target was not Nuremberg. The crew had been there twice before. A long, dreary eight-hour trip. The last time, McLauchlan had shot down a Dornier 217 night fighter which had attacked and damaged their Halifax Mark III N-NAN. The pilot and the navigator had both been awarded the DFC for this action.

As the day wore on at the Skipton Bridge airfield, McLauchlan could not suppress the presentiment that the crew would not be coming back from Nuremberg. So much so that, after a briefing at which the aircrews were assured of cloud cover all the way into the target and most of the way back again, he gave away all his shirts and a new uniform to another crew not on operations that night. Having done this and checked and cleaned the guns in his turret, he settled down to an unusually hearty ops tea of four poached eggs.

'Somehow I knew it was to be my last meal in England,' he recalls.

Not that there was any apparent reason for gloom. They were an experienced and combat-tested crew who had previously been with No. 419 Squadron in Main Force and before that with No. 405 Squadron in the Pathfinder Force. Moreover, with twenty-nine operations safely behind them, they had succeeded, so far, in beating the formidable odds against the average crew's chances of completing a tour of thirty trips.

The only alien factor was that they would have a second pilot flying with them that night, a new pilot on the squadron who was being given a taste of operational experience before taking his own crew on their first operation. (Except at training units, Bomber Command Lancasters and Halifaxes were not fitted with dual flying controls and did not carry a permanent second pilot. This function was, in part, fulfilled by the flight engineer.)

After chuckling over a somewhat bawdy story told them by the padre who had come out to farewell them and wish them luck at their aircraft, they could no longer delay the inevitable. Climbing into their darkened Halifax they once more went through the familiar drills and rituals which had carried them through twenty-nine trips before.

Crossing the English coast and then the French coast, McLauchlan watchfully rotated his rear turret in the bright, unclouded moonlight of enemy air space, scanning from side to side of the sky.

On the way to the target, the long way in, McLauchlan saw many combats but actually witnessed only about six British bombers going down out of control. So far, so good. With the bomb-doors open for the run-in to the target aiming-point and with the intercom silent except for the voice of Les Milward, the bomb aimer, giving Chris Nielsen, the pilot, corrections on the bombing run, McLauchlan was totally unprepared for what was about to happen so suddenly and so violently.

Confusion in the target area was the main recollection of Flying Officer H. B. Mackinnon, a navigator in 'B' Flight of No. 57 Squadron, East Kirkby, one of the No. 5 Group formations in Lincolnshire.

Mackinnon's crew were a typical Bomber Command amalgam of ranks, a contradictory state of affairs which somehow seemed to work well, certainly in the air: Sergeant R. E. Walker, pilot; Flying Officer K. E. Bly, RCAF, bomb aimer; Sergeant E. Chung, flight engineer; Sergeant R. A. Hammersley, wireless air gunner; Flying Officer T. Quayle, mid-upper gunner; Sergeant W. Carver, rear gunner.

Of the raid in its entirety, Mackinnon remembered very little. 'In any case,' he wryly pointed out, 'the navigator, thank goodness, saw but little.'

The London-born navigator and his crew were airborne from East Kirkby's flarepath in Lancaster N-NAN, Serial No. ND 560, at 2210. The bomb-load was 10 500 pounds. They had been briefed to expect Wanganui coloured sky markers positioned over the target by Oboe-equipped blind-marking Mosquitoes. The reality of what was to happen a few hours later was something else again.

'As we were turning at 50° 30′ North, 10° 40′ East to go south to the target,' Mackinnon recalls, 'Bly, our Canadian bomb aimer, reported that he could see target-indicator flares going down. As I estimated we were more than sixty miles from the target I said that he must have darned good eyesight. He insisted they were there, pretty well on our starboard bow, and we were going past them. The pilot then plaintively asked me where we were to go. H2S was behaving well and I insisted that we go straight on. Nevertheless, I was relieved when the bomb aimer duly reported further TI flares straight ahead, where they were supposed to be. Later we learned that, in error, PFF had marked Schweinfurt.'

Between five and ten minutes ahead of the Main Force stream in which Mackinnon was having such a confusing time, Wing Commander S. P. Daniels, DSO, DFC and

bar, RAFVR, was flying a Lancaster, s-SUGAR, of No. 35
Squadron, a Pathfinder Force unit of No. 8 Group.

Daniels has a clear recollection of the Nuremberg opera-
tion. It was his sixty-sixth in four tours of heavy bomber
operations. His crew included Pilot Officer Copp, Flight
Lieutenant Wilkinson, Flight Sergeant Moffat, Warrant
Officer Campbell and Second Lieutenant Wang, a Free
Norwegian Air Force officer.

Apologizing for being unable to remember who occupied
which crew positions in his Lancaster on the night of
Nuremberg, Wing Commander Daniels explained:

'As CO, I was not allowed my own crew and usually took
one where the captain was sick or on leave or else I just made
up a crew of odd bods from around the place or sometimes I
took a new crew. This system was unpopular with all but a
necessary evil.

'There is no reference in my log book to having carried out
a night-flying test. Presumably I made someone else do this
for me. As CO there was a lot of work to do: preparing the
briefing that I would give the squadron, studying weather
reports and talking of tactics with the Air Officer Commanding, and Group, on the scrambler telephone link-up,
checking maximum number of squadron aircraft and crews
available, checking the route with the navigation officer,
signals arrangements with the signals leader and giving a
a separate briefing to whatever crew I was taking with me.
Correct loading of bombs and fuel also had to be checked.'

Having heard, and given, so many briefings during his
long operational career, Daniels could not recall in detail
the briefing which he gave No. 35 Squadron. However, the
reason for the long straight leg across the Rhine east to the
target was because of the distance to be covered. Intelligence,
furthermore, had claimed that southern Germany was not as
heavily defended as the more frequently attacked targets
areas of central and northern Germany.

'For once,' Daniels recalls, 'I was not Master Bomber. I
probably took off first with the rest of the squadron behind
me at thirty-second intervals, about five to ten minutes
ahead of Main Force.

'I can still vividly recall that as soon as we crossed the

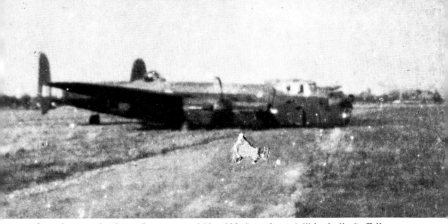

One that got back—a Lancaster of No. 622 Squadron, Mildenhall, Suffolk, which crash-landed at Woodbridge, on the Sussex coast, with landing-gear retracted, a fire in the forward fuselage, failure of the electrical system and a starboard engine out of action.   *L. H. Gregson*

Nuremberg damage to Flying Officer H. T. Forrest's Lancaster WS-V of No. 9 Squadron, Bardney, Lincolnshire. The rear turret is beyond the Elsan portable toilet at top of photograph. The step at left is to the fuselage entrance door.   *From the Garbett/Goulding Collection, photo: R. J. Harris*

Lancaster GI-J of No. 622 Squadron, Mildenhall, Suffolk, prior to take-off for Nuremberg. This aircraft survived to fly a hundred operations.
L. H. Gregson, copied by M. Garbett

Lancaster DX-A of No. 57 Squadron, East Kirkby, Lincolnshire, flown by Pilot Officer K. D. Smith. *Copyright: H. Welland*

Six of the crew of Lancaster GT-X of No. 156 Squadron, Warboys, a Pathfinder Force unit—Flying Officer S. H. Johnson, RAAF, navigator/radar-set operator; Squadron Leader Les Glasspool, DFC, navigator-plotter; W. H. J. Love, RAAF, DFC, DFM, rear gunner; Sergeant Truman, RAF, flight engineer; Arthur Irwin, RAF, mid-upper gunner; and Squadron Leader D. M. Walbourn, RAF, DSO, DFC. *S. H. Johnson*

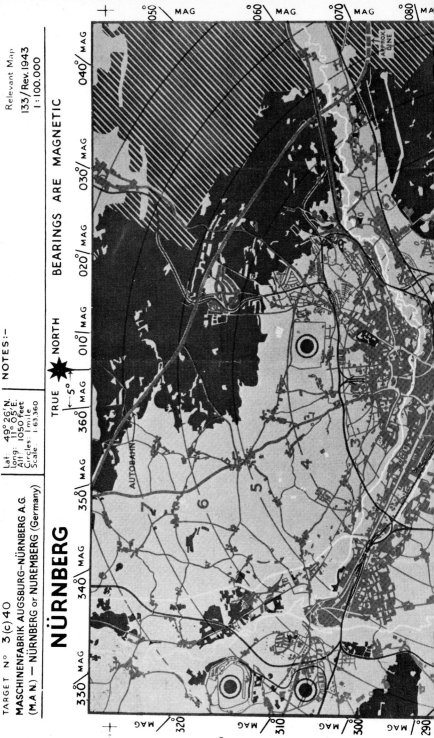

Detailed RAF radar target map of Nuremberg for Bomber Command navigators t
compare with the pictures on their H2S radar screens. The scale is 1:63,360 with ever
inch between the concentric circles representing a mile on the ground.

AUTOBAHN

APPROX. LINE 7

UNCONFIRMED WOODS:— 25 Sept 1943

MAG 100° / MAG 110° / MAG 120° / MAG 130° / MAG 140° / MAG 150° / MAG 160° / MAG 170° / MAG 180° / MAG 190° / MAG 200° / MAG 210° / MAG 220° / MAG 230° / MAG 240° / MAG 250° / MAG 260° / MAG 270°

TRUE N

NURNBERG

(a) W/V at   Ft. FLARE Ht. =   (d) FLARE DRIFT =

(b) TIME OF FALL =   (e) M.F.Co. =

(c) FORWARD TRAVEL =   (f) T.A.S. (Mean B.C.) =

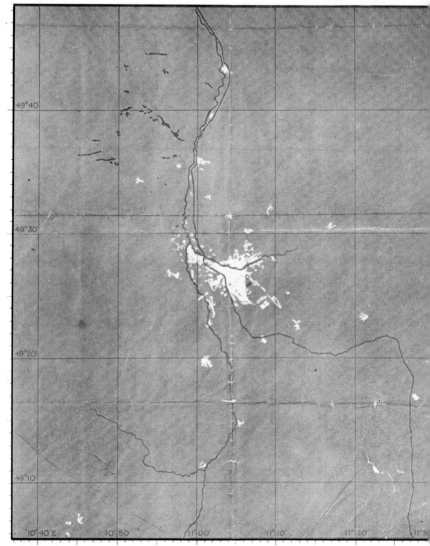

18th JANUARY

SCALE 1:250,000

RAF radar target map of Nuremberg issued on 18 January 1944 showing
what a Bomber Command navigator could expect to see on his thirty-mile
H2S radar screen on approach to the target.

DATE OF SORTIE	TARGET	IDENTIFICATION OF TARGET	PHOTOGRAPHIC RESULT	NAVIGATION	REMARKS	NO. OF SORTIES.
1944 15/16th MARCH.	~~BERLIN~~ STUTTGART	–	–	–	2nd Pilot (LECONFIELD) 2nd Pilot	S / SA /
26/27th MARCH.	ESSEN	Green T/I's.	Cloud 10/10ths. Photo not plotted.	Average.		52
30/31st. MARCH.	NURNBERG	Red T/I's.	Mainly cloud and few fire tracks. Not plotted.	Average.		SB /
9/10th April	LILLE	Red T/I's	Bombing frame shows smoke and T/I's plotted, no ground detail	Average.		S
10/11th April	TERGNIER	Two Red T/Is and two Greens.	5th frame shows T/I's and ground detail.	Average.	Bombs hung up over target and were jettisoned safe at 50N/0030E. Wing] bombs went over target.	S
18/19th April.	TERGNIER	Red and Green	Bombing Frame N/P. 7th 3,600 yds 217° from A/P.	Good average		S
20/21st April	OTTIGNIES.	Four Reds tk.	Plotted 900yds from A/P. 347° N.N.E.	Average.		S.
22/23rd April.	DUSSELDORF	Red T/Is.	Intensity of fire tracks.	Good Average.		S.
24/25th April.	KARLSRUHE.	Reds with yellow stars.	Intensity of fire tracks.	Average		S. /
26/27th April.	VILLENEUVE ST GEORGES.	T/I Green, Red (&) Spot fires.	Plotted 2,400 from A/P.	Average.		S 1/3

Assessment of sorties carried out, including Nuremberg, by Flight Sergeant
P. E. Christiansen, RCAF, and his crew in Halifax Mark III, coded EY-A, of
No. 78 Squadron, Breighton, Yorkshire.   *D. G. Davidson*

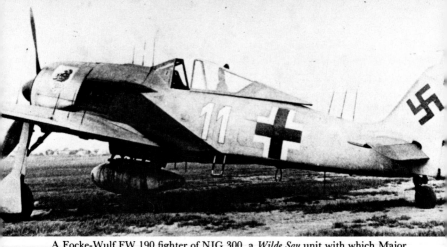

A Focke-Wulf FW 190 fighter of NJG 300, a *Wilde Sau* unit with which Major Karl-Friedrich Mueller became the highest-scoring, single-engine night-fighter pilot of the Luftwaffe, with a total of thirty-one victories. Fortunately for Bomber Command he did not fly on the night of 30 March 1944. The antenna arrays were for the FuG radar search equipment which this unit evaluated during interception operations at night. *Hans Rossbach, Koblenz, Germany*

Nuremberg raid report on Halifax EY-A of No. 78 Squadron, Breighton, Yorkshire, from the base to Headquarters, 4 Group. *D. G. Davidson*

A - F/S. CHRISTIANSE'

INT./OPS
C.O.

HOM V 9RE 9RE 4/1
T

FROM 9REIGHTON 011000A
TO H.Q.4 GROUP
INFO HOLME
SECRET OOX BT

SECTION 'A'   RAID REPORT 11 30/31ST MARCH 1944
                     ───────────────────────────────────

4 GROUP
30/31 ST MARCH 1944   7R/A
48 X 30 INC 480 X 4 INC   9REIGHTON 11
60 X 4 LB 'X' PFF INCS   HALIFAX III
MONICA I. API.   F/S CHRISTIANSEN (2)
NURNBERG SECOND   A/C LANDED AT FORD

SECTION 'C'
──────────
(1) NURNBERG
(2) 8/10THS CLOUD OVER T/A . VISIBILITY VERY GOOD. VISIBILITY
    POOR ON RETURN.
(4) 0123 20,000: 165 (M) 160 I.A.S.
(3) RED 'T/1's.
(6) MEAN CENTRE OF APPROX 10 RED T/1's
(8) VERY LARGE FIRES SEEN ALL OVER T/A. EXPLOSIONS AT INTERVALS.
    SEEN T/1'S SEEN TO BE FAIRLY WELL CONCENTRATED.
(10) RED T/1'S SEEN AT AACHEN
(11) (A) A.P.I.
(12) A.H.B. 1000 1/4/44
BT 011000A

M.K.M. K
IMI

enemy coast there was evidence of the greatest fighter opposition I had ever contacted. Fighter flares were being dropped
to mark our route and scarecrows, simulating exploding
aircraft, were being fired into the bomber stream.

'My crew, who were not very experienced, were rather
shaken by the sight of large numbers of our aircraft being
attacked and shot down.

'Since I always insisted on no intercom chatter and strict
silence so that our gunners could give warning of attacks on
ourselves I instructed the navigator to stop logging sightings
of aircraft being shot down as there were so many occurring
that he would not have been able to carry out his normal
work of navigation.'

Wing Commander Daniels was attacked once by night
fighters on the way into the danger area.

'I did a lot of cork-screwing up and down, four or five
hundred feet, with continual steep banking, for periods of
four or five minutes, whenever I felt fighters were near.'

Such was the benefit of long operational experience that a
pilot like Daniels could sense the imminence of attack.

His arrival over the target was to prove to be something of
an anti-climax.

Due probably to the fact that he was shot down over Amiens
ten days later, Sergeant H. J. Beddis, RAF, a flight engineer
in 'B' Flight of No. 103 Squadron, a No. 1 Group united
based at Elsham Wolds, Lincolnshire, recalled very little of
the events of that night.

Strangely yet typically, for a prolonged air battle at night
had many shifting facets, Howard Beddis spent eight and a
half hours in the jump-seat alongside his pilot, Pilot Officer
Armstrong, RNZAF, that night and did not see one single
enemy fighter. He remembers only that the concentration of
flak around the target was 'fairly heavy'.

The Birmingham flight engineer's Lancaster Mark III,
Serial No. JB 732, returned entirely unscathed to its dispersal
at Elsham Wolds.

Another Lincolnshire-based airman, RAF navigator Pilot
Officer D. S. Richardson, of No. 50 Squadron, Skellingthorpe,

in No. 5 Group, retained a limited yet accurate recollection of the operation.

At 1930 he sat down to a pre-operations meal as did the rest of his crew: Pilot Officer R. H. Lloyd, pilot; Flight Sergeant L. T. Dewhirst, bomb aimer; Sergeant M. Avenell, flight engineer; Flight Sergeant 'Paddy' Hewson, wireless air gunner; Sergeant A. McCarthy, mid-upper gunner; Sergeant N. F. Bacon, rear gunner.

Main briefing was at 2030. Concentration points for the Main Force bomber stream were to be first fix Home and at positions *B*, *C*, the target, and positions *E*, *F*, and *G*.

As navigator of his crew's Lancaster UN-F, Serial No. LL 842, Pilot Officer Richardson's responsibility to his captain was to have the aircraft over the target during the 180 seconds which would elapse between 0110 and 0113. The last 'time over target' report was at 0122. Bombing would be from 23 000 feet.

Pathfinders would drop red target-indicator flares as a route marker at 50° 46′ North, 06° 06′ East. The target would be marked by the Pathfinder Force with Newhaven illuminating flares and green target-indicators with salvoes of red and green followed by reds. Wanganui marking would consist of red flares with yellow stars.

Pathfinders would also carry out spoofs with green target-indicators on Cologne and red target-indicators on Kassel.

For the guidance of the outward-bound bomber stream the beams of two searchlights would be crossed at 10 000 feet over Lowestoft on the Norfolk coast between 2300 and 2330.

On their return, a single searchlight would be shining at Selsey Bill, elevated to 70° on a heading of 350°, between 0410 and 0530. This simple but effective navigational aid, welcoming the bombers back across the English coast, would be appreciated most of all by aircraft limping home with battle damage and killed or wounded crew members.

Despite all the careful planning, however, Richardson noted early in the night that the forecast winds given out at briefing were not as forecast. By 07° East, consequently, the Main Force stream of bombers was north of track and dangerously close to the Pathfinders' diversionary spoof at Cologne and the spoof simulated Luftwaffe fighter flare at

08° East. Not for the first time, the weather had betrayed Bomber Command and the stream of Lancasters and Halifaxes was drifting closer to the very baits, the spoofs, which had been laid to attract the Luftwaffe's night fighters.

'Our rear gunner reported many combats in this area,' the navigator recalled. 'They were too numerous to log. We altered course to avoid the Ruhr so probably avoided the main fighter activity.'

Pilot Officer Lloyd, Richardson's skipper, was actually able to follow vapour trails streamed in the moonlight by the Pathfinders in the direction of the target which Lancaster UN-F was to bomb at 0111.

Perhaps one of the briefest comments recorded on the operation was to come from Pilot Officer P. E. Plowright, RAF, an 'A' Flight pilot with No. 9 Squadron, Bardney, Lincolnshire, in No. 5 Group.

After eight hours airborne to Nuremberg and back in his Lancaster Mark I J-JIG, Serial No. W 4964, he made the following entry in his pilot's log book:

'My 18th operation. Target, Nuremberg, Wanganui marking. Fighters active on route but target OK. Marking scattered. Ninety-nine aircraft lost.'

In another Lancaster of No. 5 Group—JO-B, of No. 463 Squadron, Waddington—the flight engineer, Sergeant Eric Morrey, from Cheshire, was the only Englishman in a crew of Australians: Pilot Officer Charlie Cassell, pilot; Flight Sergeant Victor Brill, navigator; Flight Sergeant Tom Morris, bomb aimer; Flight Sergeant Max Merry, wireless air gunner; Pilot Officer Ian Paul, mid-upper gunner; Flight Sergeant Max Milner, rear gunner.

On arrival at JO-B's dispersal point that evening Sergeant Morrey, as flight engineer, was too busy to worry overmuch about the far distant target for that night.

After checking that the pitot head cover was off and that all engine cowlings and inspection panels were secure he climbed into the aircraft and made his way forward to his jump-seat alongside the pilot, Pilot Officer Cassell, checking that first-aid kits, hand fire-extinguishers and portable oxygen sets were in position, that emergency escape hatches were secure and that all pyrotechnics were safely stowed. Fuel booster pumps were then tested, carburettors primed and fuel tank contents noted. With Cassell he then carried out engine controls check, cockpit check and pre-flight drill.

One by one the four engines were then started and when they were warmed up and running satisfactorily, the hydraulic system was tested to operate flaps, bomb-doors and turrets. Oxygen and intercom systems were also tested with the rest of their crew at their stations.

On arrival at the runway holding-point, Morrey and Cassell made a final check of engine temperatures and pressures. All engines were then run-up for the last time. Leaning forward, Cassell set the directional gyro on his instrument panel to a zero heading for take-off. They were ready to go.

Finally, at 2220, an Aldis lamp flashed green in the darkness and JO-B rolled out onto the runway and lined up for takeoff. The take-off was routine with Cassell opening up all four throttles to full power but leading slightly with the port outer throttle to counteract the Lancaster's tendency to swing to port.

At 800 feet over the darkened Lincolnshire countryside, Morrey returned the flaps to normal—25° of flap was the recommended setting for take-off—and JO-B, a Lancaster Mark I with Rolls-Royce Merlin XXII engines, settled down to a steady climb at 145 mph with a maximum fuel load and the usual bomb-load of a 4000-pound blockbuster and containers of clustered four-pound incendiaries.

'Strict silence was observed now,' Morrey recalls, 'unless to indicate any incident which required attention and this was only broken at regular intervals with Charlie Cassell checking with each member of the crew.'

At 19 500 feet, Cassell levelled out at a speed of 165 mph which was maintained during the outward flight.

Morrey could tell when they reached the enemy coast:

'There was the usual moderate flak coming up with tracer in front of the aircraft and fading away again in the darkness. Searchlights were occasionally picking out aircraft but we were fortunate and not troubled. Tom Morris, the bomb aimer, and I were now putting bundles of silver paper called window down the chute to upset the enemy radar system.

'It was very cold now inside the aircraft and the hot-air system seemed to have no effect at this height.

'Eventually, a glow in the distance came into sight and I knew it was fires burning at the target. As the sky came brighter with the glow from these fires, other aircraft became visible above us and on each side of us, all flying in the same direction and from now on a special check was made to see if any aircraft were above us and directly in line with us as we were quickly approaching the target.'

Not so fortunate on their way into Germany were the RAF crew of another 5 Group Lancaster, V-VICTOR, from No. 9 Squadron, Bardney, Lincolnshire: Pilot Officer H. T. Forrest, pilot; Sergeant Harwood, navigator; Sergeant Hutton, flight engineer; Sergeant D. McCauley, wireless air gunner; Flight Sergeant Utting, mid-upper gunner; Sergeant Pinchin, rear gunner.

Their aircraft was a Lancaster Mark I, Serial No. DV 395, with Rolls-Royce Merlin XXII engines.

The 10 672-pound bomb-load consisted of the 4000-pound 'cookie', six containers each holding 150 4-pound incendiaries, five containers holding twelve 30-pound incendiaries, one container holding sixteen 30-pound incendiaries and one container holding eight 30-pound incendiaries. It was a bomb-load destined never to reach its target.

Pilot Officer Forrest recalls an initially uneventful flight along the route south over France with a turn to port to cross the Rhine between Koblenz and Bonn. The fact that there was a good half-moon and a clear sky, however, was something that had concerned him early, a concern soon to be justified.

He has a clear recollection of subsequent events:

'As we approached the Rhine it was evident that there was considerable enemy fighter activity in the area with the result that the frequency of our "bank and search" was increased and the wireless operator asked to keep careful watch on Monica.

'Without warning we were hit from below and astern by cannon-fire and I immediately began corkscrewing. The enemy aircraft, a Ju 88, was seen to break away to port. Our aircraft was on fire in the rear bomb-bay or rear fuselage and the intercom was dead.

'I gave orders to the flight engineer to open bomb-doors and jettison the load. This being done the fire still persisted, so I decided the best thing to do was dive.'

(Diving speed of the Lancaster was limited to 360 mph. At or about this speed, according to AP 2062C-PN, *Pilot's Notes for Lancaster Mark III*, controls tended to stiffen up. So did the occupants, as the author's flying instructor at No. 1654 Lancaster Conversion Unit was once heard to observe.)

After a short time in the dive Forrest had blown out the fire and he levelled off at about 14 000 feet.

'By this time,' he said, 'the wireless operator had rectified the fault in the intercom and asked if he could go aft to look at Flight Sergeant Utting, the mid-upper gunner, who had climbed down from his turret and collapsed by the main spar. I agreed and then checked that the rear gunner was OK. The wireless operator then called up and reported that the mid-upper gunner was dead.

'The aircraft appeared to respond normally to controls and it was felt that as there was no power for the turrets the best course of action would be to climb on track and follow the Main Force to the target and return with them to base. This we did without further incident.'

Meanwhile, another No. 9 Squadron Lancaster from Bardney, F-FOX of 'A' Flight, was settling down on the long haul to Nuremberg.

So far it had been a quiet night for the crew: Flight Lieutenant D. Pearce, RAF, pilot; Flying Officer J. E. Logan, RCAF, navigator; Flying Officer W. Pearson, RCAF, bomb aimer; Sergeant Howe, RAF, flight engineer; Sergeant J. S. Maclean, mid-upper gunner; Warrant Officer 'Sonny' Thomas, RAAF, rear gunner and Flight Sergeant W. Doran, RAF, wireless air gunner.

According to the log book of the Scots-born mid-upper gunner, Sergeant Stuart, F-FOX had taken off at 2205. Crossing the enemy coast, Stuart observed that there was a quarter-moon and visibility was good, probably too good for night operations. Yet, perhaps because F-FOX was being flown slightly off track, Stuart and his crew enjoyed an entirely uneventful trip to the target.

Not so was it for Flight Sergeant R. B. Callaway, RCAF, who had volunteered to fly as a 'spare bod' in the rear turret of Lancaster OW-N, in 'B' Flight of No. 426 Squadron, Linton-on-Ouse, in No. 6 Group. His pilot was Flight Lieutenant Shedd.

'We were told at briefing that the diversions towards Berlin would draw any fighters away from us,' Flight Sergeant Callaway recalled. 'However, it sure seemed that Jerry had all our turning-points marked well in advance. My buddy at the time, Sergeant Shoquist, had walked out to the dispersal area where he said goodbye and added that he wouldn't be seeing me again. As a matter of fact I wasn't to see him again until 1946 in Vancouver, BC, when, by comparing stories, it turned out that I had seen him shot down.

'North of Nuremberg I spotted a Ju 88 firing at a Lancaster on our port beam and shooting it down. This was about 0100. The Ju 88 then hauled around to starboard and was coming at us when we let go a burst at him. He veered off and tackled another Lancaster on our starboard beam which blew up. This was Shoquist's aircraft.'

Callaway remembered that his aircraft ran into spirited enemy opposition as soon as it crossed the French coast:

'I believe this was the first time the Germans had used scarecrows fired up into the bomber stream. I must say they were a stupendous sight; however I can't really see that they scared anyone. I know that our count of aircraft shot down seemed high at first until we surmised that something had to be afoot because they were bursting with such nice rainbow colours on contact with the ground.'

In the clear moonlit sky, Callaway and his crew were able to count an unusually high number of parachute canopies opening up in the bomber stream.

For the lucky ones, the Nuremberg operation was also a clear and convincing case of the early bird being rewarded for its enterprise. This was certainly to be so for Pilot Officer F. Collis, the Lancaster pilot in 'B' Flight of the author's own squadron, No. 207, based at Spilsby, Lincolnshire, in No. 5 Group.

Pilot Officer Collis, born at Megantic, Quebec Province, Canada, and a police constable with the London metropolitan police force before enlisting in the Royal Air Force, was to recall Nuremberg only as a trip that, for once, 'went smoothly'.

After going through the usual pre-operations routine—a night-flying test of the crew's aircraft, specialized briefings by flight commanders to pilots and by leaders of navigation, bombing, gunnery, signals and engineering sections with a final main briefing for all crews gathered together—Collis took off in his Lancaster EM-V at 2200.

With him as he lifted off, with four black-snouted Merlin engines howling, were: Sergeant Griffiths, his Welsh navigator; Flying Officer Essery, a Canadian from Toronto, bomb aimer; Sergeant Atkins, a local from Lincolnshire and the crew's flight engineer; Sergeant Fox, from Tunbridge, wireless air gunner; Sergeant Topple, from London's Welwyn Garden City, mid-upper gunner; Sergeant Skinner, a Kentishman, rear gunner.

They were the first No. 207 Squadron crew to take off that night from the flare path at Spilsby near the railway linking Boston and Louth, inland from Skegness on the Wash. The reason for their early departure was that they were to fly with the Pathfinder Force, ahead of the first wave of the Main Force bomber stream. This, as it turned out, was to be a major factor in Collis and his crew keeping out of trouble as the full fury of the violent counter-attack by the Luftwaffe developed behind them while they ranged ahead of the first wave, hard on the heels of PFF.

Climbing and circling over Spilsby and the dwindling pattern of its airfield lighting system, Collis set course thirty-eight minutes after take-off on a heading of 141° Magnetic.

With truly policeman-like precision he recalled the succession of that night's events as he saw them, strapped tightly into his armour-plated pilot's seat:

'At 2304 the bombs were fused and navigation lights

turned off.' (This was always the signal to a crew that they were about to penetrate enemy air space for, in England's crowded war-time skies, mid-air collisions at night were an occupational hazard. Against this risk navigation lights were minimally helpful for without them a friendly Lancaster or Halifax in the bomber stream was potentially as dangerous as a Luftwaffe night fighter.)

'At 2315, over the North Sea, we commenced windowing. At 2327 we crossed the enemy coast at 20 000 feet. At 2346 we passed to the west of Brussels and had by then climbed to 21 000 feet, our height for bombing.

'Prior to bombing I can recall much more enemy activity behind us along our track than was usual but we were, ourselves, having it very easy. We had a detailed view of the whole affair with no possible chance of harm coming to us but it was obviously coming to others. In the distance, too, we could see PFF dropping the target-indicator markers for the diversionary spoofs, as briefed, on Cologne and Kassel.'

Away to the south of Collis's base at Spilsby, another Lancaster had taken off that night from Mildenhall, in Suffolk, navigated by London-born Sergeant E. C. Hazelwood, 'B' Flight, No. 622 Squadron, in No. 3 Group.

With the exception of the Canadian bomb aimer, Flying Officer Burnett, the crew of the Lancaster u-uncle were all English and all non-commissioned: Flight Sergeant McQueen, pilot; Sergeant Mattingly, flight engineer; Sergeant Blakes, wireless air gunner; Sergeant Quinlan, mid-upper gunner; Flight Sergeant Chivers, rear gunner.

Conscious of his responsibilities as a navigator and anxious to do his job well, Sergeant Hazelwood had, once airborne, previously always kept himself shut off from activity outside the aircraft so that he could concentrate on his navigation (a task which he did not find any easier when he was suffering from air-sickness as a result of evasive corkscrewing by his pilot, McQueen, to escape enemy attack). On this night, however, in view of the crew's comments on the intercom, he left his navigation table to look out for once to see just what was happening.

Near Bonn, south of the fabled but infamous industrial

complex of the Ruhr, what Hazelwood saw was not reassuring:

'A lot of our aircraft seemed to be drifting north into the Ruhr defences as I saw a lot of activity over the Ruhr with searchlights and gunfire. I thought at the time that the winds might have changed and drifted a lot of the aircraft off track.'

From his position in the nose of the Lancaster, prone above the forward escape hatch in the floor, the Canadian bomb aimer, Flying Officer Burnett, remarked how bright the moon was and that he could see 'for miles'.

The gunners and the rest of the crew who were looking out all agreed that it was 'a lovely night', with nobody voicing the thought that was in all their minds, 'for German night fighters'.

After passing the high flak glittering over the misted gloom of the Ruhr Valley it was Hazelwood's time to feel that his aircraft was either being followed or being waited for.

'In front of us,' he recalled, 'anti-aircraft shells were being shot into the air and, on exploding, looked like aircraft being shot down.'

With a blithely British calmness that no doubt would have infuriated the sweating Luftwaffe flak gunners far below, Hazelwood added, almost as an afterthought, 'I suppose this was to upset aircrew morale.'

On several occasions Sergeant Quinlan in the two-gun mid-upper turret and Flight Sergeant Chivers in the four-gun rear turret saw enemy aircraft but held their fire in case the muzzle-flashes from their guns betrayed the Lancaster's position in the bomber stream.

'Our orders were to bomb the target, not to engage in fighting enemy aircraft,' Hazelwood recalls. Though unlikely to have inspired paeans of patriotic praise, this tactic nevertheless had about it a certain cold and brutal logic which was entirely in keeping with the bloody business of bombing Germany out of the war.

On the long leg eastward across the bitterly contested line of the Rhine and on to the target, the gunners of Hazelwood's Lancaster were to see many more enemy aircraft including Dornier Do 17s, probably flare-droppers and observers plotting the track of the bomber stream, and many Messerschmitt Me 210 fighters.

None of them, though, were to stop Hazelwood's Lancaster from reaching Nuremberg.

Flying Officer Fred Stetson, rear gunner of another Lancaster, was subsequently reported in the British *Weekly News* as recalling:

'I had been dreading the next mission. I can laugh at it now but during the war I was very superstitious. I had, for instance, Saint Christopher medals hanging all over my turret.

'This was my 24th operation. The serial number of our Lanc. was KK204, my personal service number was 149109 which added up to 24 and D is the fourth letter of the alphabet. And remember it was 1944. That figure four seemed to haunt me.'

As it happened, Stetson's number nearly came up on Nuremberg.

In his rear turret festooned with Saint Christopher medals, Stetson had a quiet trip into Germany until the target area was reached and the straight-and-level bombing run commenced, with heavy flak coming up.

'One engine was hit and a petrol tank holed,' he said. 'We dropped our bombs bang-on, weaved like mad and skated out of the area.

'Soon, a fighter attacked. I tried to swivel my guns. The turret would not work. I could turn it a little to port—not at all to starboard. Luckily the attack was from the port side and I was able to direct a stream of .303s in his general direction. I yelled to the wireless operator for help in freeing the turret. The fighter turned away. Was I relieved! But the wireless operator couldn't get the turret working. I fumbled on the floor for any obstruction. Guess what? One of those Saint Christopher medals I was so fond of had fallen during the weaving and jammed between the stationary and moving parts of the turret.'

With or without the help of Saint Christopher, Flying Officer Stetson and his crew returned safely to their base.

On his way to Nuremberg that night from the RAAF base at

Waddington, in Lincolnshire, was Squadron Leader A. W. Doubleday, DFC, a friend of No. 463's Brill who was somewhere in the bomber stream with him.

For a long time, in terms of war-time associations, Doubleday and Brill had shared a joint 'Tweedledum and Tweedledee' community of service careers since they had left their farms in the peaceful Riverina district of New South Wales and joined the RAAF in Australia in 1940.

Selected for pilot training and, after graduation as multi-engine pilots, posted to the United Kingdom on attachment to the RAF, they had duly arrived in Bomber Command, amongst the first of what was to become a torrent of British Commonwealth aircrews.

Now Brill and Doubleday were both flying Lancasters on different squadrons but from the same base, Waddington, each with the rank of Squadron Leader, each commanding a flight and each wearing the ribbon of the DFC.

Before the war was over they were both destined to become wing commanders, to win the DSO and to lead their own Lancaster squadrons—Brill, No. 467 and Doubleday No. 61.

With the exception of the flight engineer, Sergeant Slome, Squadron Leader Doubleday's crew for Nuremberg were all commissioned: Flight Lieutenant Abbott, navigator; Flying Officer Nugent, bomb aimer; Flying Officer Sinnamon, wireless air gunner; Flying Officer Buchanan, mid-upper gunner; Flying Officer Taylor, rear gunner.

Doubleday's Lancaster, from 'B' Flight, No. 467 (RAAF) Squadron, was coded x-xray, Serial No. LL 843.

Apart from the fact that his DR compass went unserviceable before take-off which meant he had to fly all night by careful monitoring of the P6 compass, it seemed to Doubleday that the Nuremberg operation was similar to another on which heavy losses had recently been suffered by Bomber Command—Leipzig, on the night of 19 February, when seventy-eight aircraft failed to return.

'There was a three-quarter moon,' said Doubleday, commenting on Nuremberg as he remembered it. 'Condensation trails were present for the major part of the period over the Continent. I believe this was above 16 000 feet. The winds from the north were not as strong as forecast.'

He recalled 'a good deal' of fighter activity from the time of crossing the enemy coast in to the target but little, if anything, from there on. He also recalled, in a general way, that most of the aircraft that crashed were immediately south of Cologne.

(Squadron Leader Doubleday's experienced observations confirmed reports by other aircrews that the Luftwaffe night-fighter force appeared to have massed in strength for a violent and determined counter-attack at a point near where the track of the bomber stream crossed the Rhine, south of Cologne, between Bonn and Koblenz.)

4   The Target

Long before the tense and worried crews of the first wave of Lancasters and Halifaxes in the Main Force bomber stream had opened their bomb-doors over Nuremberg—indeed, long before the lone Mosquitoes of the probing Pathfinder Force had even located, illuminated and marked the aiming-point in Nuremberg—the RAF attack was already in jeopardy, if not mortal peril.

It was all happening just as Squadron Leader Billy Brill of No. 463 (RAAF) Squadron and his similarly battle-experienced flying contemporaries of Bomber Command had grimly predicted it would.

The Germans had not swallowed the bait so carefully laid for them by the Bomber Command planners who had built into the night's operations the complex series of diversionary spoofs—a sizeable mine-laying sortie by fifty Halifaxes across the North Sea to the Heligoland Bight, the red TIs at Aachen and the red and green TIs at Cologne and Kassel. The equally combat-seasoned staff officers, commanders, operations officers, controllers and aircrews of the Luftwaffe night-fighter force had duly observed and assessed the line of bogus attacks strung along a ghost track which diverged tangentially from that which Bomber Command was actually following eastward to Nuremberg. But the Luftwaffe had not assumed that the RAF was in fact heading past Kassel to Berlin or towards the arc of other possible targets to the west of the sprawling capital on the Spree—Hanover, Braunschweig, Magdeburg, Halle, Leipzig or Chemnitz.

Bomber Command's diversionary spoofs were quickly

confirmed as such when the aircraft involved were positively identified not as heavy bombers of the Main Force stream but as Mosquitoes. This was revealed when the German radar system monitors reported that the aircraft over Aachen, Cologne and Kassel were not producing the tell-tale electronic emissions characteristically associated with the H2S blind bombing and navigation aid used by most of the Lancasters and Halifaxes of the Main Force squadrons. (Radar-equipped German night fighters had for some time been able to home on the H2S transmissions—with disastrous results for the unsuspecting Lancasters and Halifaxes concerned.)

Such was the irony and degree of much of the technological boffinry associated with the unending struggle between the two opposing air forces that the development of a radar aid which greatly improved the RAF's all-weather bombing and navigation capability should have been 'turned around' and eagerly exploited by the Luftwaffe as a consistently accurate device for tracking and shooting down the H2S-equipped British bombers.

Once the Aachen-Cologne-Kassel spoofs and the Heligoland Bight diversion had been exposed for what they were, the Luftwaffe reacted swiftly, surely and savagely. Armed now with confirmation of their suspicions the German controllers began feeding their fighters as early as possible, and as far west as possible, into the British bomber stream which had already been carefully tracked from as far back as over England by monitoring H2S emissions from the assembling bomber stream.

By a tragically counterpoised coincidence of events, twin-engined fighters of the Luftwaffe's third fighter division were massed over a radio beacon, Ida, to the south-east of where the Pathfinders' bogus red TIs had gone down over Aachen. West of the Rhine, on a line between Bonn and Koblenz, this air division's fighters slipped like a pack of wolves into a bomber stream which by now was naked under the rising moon, unescorted and virtually as exposed as if it were flying by daylight.

Progressively, other fighters joined the besieged bomber stream, some drawn by the flares dropped by German illuminator aircraft. The fighters came from Berlin, northern

Germany and from southern Germany where they had been massing over another radio beacon, Otto, east of Frankfurt and not far south of the bombers' eastward track to position *C*, near Meiningen, the turning-point for the final run to the target.

Despite the usual massive and ingenious British jamming assault on the German radar system, the Luftwaffe's night fighters were destined to have the whip hand. The moon was high, the sky was clear and, silhouetted against luminescent layers of lower cloud, every Lancaster and Halifax was trailing what looked like 'a four-lane highway' of condensation trails from its engines.

Ignoring the spoofs, the Luftwaffe controllers progressively stepped up the intrusion of fighters into the bomber stream from the assembly points over the radio beacons Ida and Otto near, respectively, Aachen and Frankfurt.

From then on, for more than 250 miles from Aachen eastward to the target, the Main Force of Lancasters and Halifaxes was to be caught in a running engagement with the fighters of the Luftwaffe. Trapped in an ambush, the victims would hurtle, spinning, to explode and burn on the ground like a line of warning beacons across the mountains, valleys, forests and rivers of southern Germany to mark the savaged but obstinate track of the bomber stream.

Like lean, grey, dappled sharks attacking a great shoal of fish, the antennae-sprouting German fighters—fresh, fuelled and armed—kept darting into the bomber stream as their controllers tracked it. Curiously, tracking had not been as easy a task as might have been expected for the treacherous, changeable March winds which had played havoc with the RAF's navigation had also, initially, baffled the Germans who for some time were uncertain about the bomber force's ultimate destination.

Indicative of the ferocity of the battle is that at one stage, between Aachen and Nuremberg, an Australian Lancaster pilot of No. 467 (RAAF) Squadron, Flight Lieutenant M. F. Smith, DFC, was to count thirty British aircraft flaming in the sky or burning on the ground.

Even by the time the Main Force Lancasters and Halifaxes finally reached Nuremberg their problems were by no means over. The Pathfinders were late and ironically, now that it was no longer needed, cloud was obscuring the city below. Long after the planned bombing time—0105 to 0122 with zero hour at 0110—hundreds of British bombers were still circling above the target, risking collision and interception, as they waited impatiently for the PFF flares to go down.

A minority of crews, their patience exhausted, would not wait any longer for the invariably 'spot on' marking by PFF, and began bombing independently. Some of them, not equipped with H2S and therefore largely dependent on the incorrectly forecast March winds for their DR navigation, drifted away to the north as they orbited what they believed to be the target and bombed Schweinfurt, fifty-five miles north-west of Nuremberg.

By the time the Pathfinders did drop their target-indicator markers on Nuremberg the normally brilliant red and green pyrotechnics were not visible because of the dense cloud over the target. The alternative sky-markers were scattered miles apart by winds reaching more than fifty miles per hour up to 20 000 feet. Those crews who kept circling the target, patiently waiting, were finally forced to bomb the PFF markers they thought most likely to be accurate.

At the best of times, let alone on a night of confusion and threat, such as this, the target area was no place to loiter.

For most bomber crews, whether they knew it or not, the target—any target—was invariably a place of traumatic experience. The target was what it was all about. For every man it was his individual baptism of war and every time it was a fresh baptism. Without the target there would have been no operation in the first place. Regardless of what did or did not happen on the way in to the target, or on the way back, the act of bombing was the psychological watershed of every operational flight. At times, it was almost like a kind of mental orgasm. Once the bombs had gone, trailing away into the night, so too had tension and even the aircraft itself seemed to give a sigh of relief. There was, perhaps, a kind of love-hate relationship between the crews and the sole reason for their operational existence, the bombs. Apart from inhibiting an aircraft's performance and so reducing its chances of survival if attacked, several tons of high explosive and incendiary bombs were unpleasant travelling companions particularly if you were being shot at. To get rid of them, finally, was possibly to live even if those at whom they were aimed did not.

After hours of flying in darkness, the cold and calculated exposure of an aircraft, its lethal pay-load and its crew of flesh, traversing an illuminated target area, was not unlike stepping out, alone and bare of defence, onto the bright stage of a vast theatre, knowing that in its gloomy auditorium unseen assassins waited, taking careful aim with deadly weapons. Often, of course, the reality was less than the implicit threat but the target remained no less a moment of truth for all that.

For most crews, other than the very brave and the very dumb, time on such a trip tended to exist as two quite separate galaxies—time before the target and time after the target. In itself, the target was a kind of emotional vacuum when mouths got dry, pulse-rates increased, sweat chilled on the small of the back, speech became staccato and even the sweep-hands of watches seem to stand still for a leaden eternity.

For some or all of these reasons, perhaps, and because of the human mind's obstinate facility for switching off and rejecting an unacceptable fact, some of the Nuremberg survivors who were questioned did not mention their transition of the target area at all. Many made only a fragmentary reference to it.

Notable exceptions included the customarily imperturbable farmer from Wagga, New South Wales, Australia, Squadron Leader Billy Brill, of No. 463 (RAAF) Squadron. As Brill flew out of cloud over the target there was a violent explosion ahead of him:

'The ball of flame accompanying the explosion was quite intense,' he said, 'and in its light a pall of black could be seen just for an instant. Almost coincidental with the explosion our aircraft bucked and vibrated. The Pathfinder Wanganui flares could be seen directly ahead so we began our bombing run. However just as we lined up, the rear gunner reported the rear turret out of action and then, as the bombs fell away, the port outer engine lost all power. I directed the flight engineer to feather the airscrew on this motor.

'The light from the Wanganui flares above the cloud was being reflected and the whole upper sky was illuminated. It was no surprise, therefore, when the mid-upper gunner (Flying Officer "Tub" Fuller, RAAF) reported an enemy fighter lining up astern to make an attack on us. The mid-upper gunner gave me a good running commentary and when we considered that the fighter was about to fire I turned towards his line of attack and his cannon-fire passed harmlessly astern. We threw a little tracer his way and he went off to find someone he could surprise. As we set course for the long run home the second motor on the port side lost all power and the prop began windmilling in the slipstream. The thought of a five-hour, or more, run home on two motors hardly raised a cheer from the crew. However, I ordered every one to check parachutes and keep them handy and then checked to see if any engine fault could be located. Nothing amiss was evident so I told the flight engineer to feather this motor also. Before he could press the feathering button there was a cough, a shower of sparks and a sheet of flame from the second sick engine and it burst into life.'

Flying Officer Gerry Girardau, RAAF, of No. 10 Squadron, and his crew arrived on time at the target with the first wave. The bombing run was normal until the bombs had gone and the bomb-doors were closed.

'At that moment I called for a corkscrew to starboard having sighted a Ju 88 on the starboard quarter,' Girardau said. 'I opened fire and as he broke away, the mid-upper gunner also opened fire. A few seconds later we observed him to be on fire and losing height rapidly. Cloud obscured him quickly.'

From his rear turret, Girardau was glad to see the last of Nuremberg.

The target was well lit up, with conditions ideal, by the time Flight Lieutenant Stephen Burrows and his crew, of No. 44 Squadron, reached it. Numerous aircraft both British and German were sighted. The run in was normal and very steady with the bomb aimer sighting on red TI markers which were visible burning on the ground.

'Unfortunately the first run was not satisfactory,' said Burrows. 'We eventually completed three runs before bombing, the aircraft and ourselves feeling very relieved to get rid of the things. Then we had the painful job of trying to take pictures and assess damage, losing height to about 10 000 feet to carry this out. During this period I happened to glance to starboard and found to my horror another Lancaster coming straight at us at exactly the same height and screamed 'Dive, dive, dive!', the skipper doing so immediately. How we missed each other is still something we discuss even now when we meet.'

During the crew's prolonged stay over the target—they were one of the last to leave the area and head for home—it was noticeable how quiet all was.

From his mid-upper turret aboard Lancaster VN-N of Skellingthorpe's No. 50 Squadron, Flight Sergeant Brian Hayes, RAAF, was to see plenty of action before he had left the target astern, for his arrival over Nuremberg was the climax of a running air battle with up to three night fighters at a time. It started with a Ju 88 passing his aircraft on a reciprocal heading and at a slightly lower altitude. With the rear gunner, Flight Sergeant Mathews, RAF, he tracked it for about 900 yards when it turned and commenced an attack.

'The next forty-five minutes was a series of running battles,' Hayes recalls, 'as we corkscrewed and fought our way into the target, dropped our bombs and fought our way out again. It appeared as if we were attacked by three Ju 88s taking it in turns to run in from the port or starboard quarters. Fortunately, they always followed a normal curve of pursuit so we had the advantage of having practised our commentary patter, our corkscrews and our deflection-shooting time and time again against this very type of attack. This enabled us to destroy two of the Ju 88s and we either damaged or perhaps discouraged the third.

'During this time we were only vaguely aware of the magnitude of the battle going on around us which was evidenced from time to time by corkscrewing bomber aircraft with fighters in pursuit, spraying tracers in the sky, and the awful red glow of burning aircraft in the air and on the ground.

'The combination of the moon period, flares, burning aircraft, fires and tracer made visibility far too good for the bombers and those of us who survived did so mostly by the grace of God, I feel.'

By contrast, Flight Sergeant John Earl, Australian navigator of the crew of Lancaster P-PETER, of Binbrook's No. 460 (RAAF) Squadron, had only the sparsest recollection of the target: 'Reference to my log-book shows there was ten-tenths cloud over the target, i.e. obscuring the target.'

In the mid-upper turret of Lancaster ZA-M from Melbourne, Yorkshire, Flying Officer Fred Stuart, RAAF, was sweating out his 'spare bod' trip as an experienced gunner with an all-RAF crew:

'Over the target the flak was particularly heavy—the heaviest I had experienced—and that included numerous trips to Happy Valley and to the Big City. Still more fighters buzzed about like flies.

'The Pathfinders had been and dropped their markers and some of the first wave of bombers had already dropped their bombs. "Bomb the greens" came the voice of the Master Bomber circling somewhere down there.

' "Straight and level" said the skipper. "I've got her," said the bomb aimer.

'Left, left, steady. Bomb doors open. Bombs away. All bombs gone. Doors closed.

' "She's all yours, driver. Let's get to hell out of here. I've got a date for breakfast in York" '

A few minutes which had seemed an eternity had passed.

'Turning off the bombing run we set course for home just a little happier than on the outward journey. Twice more we were hit by night fighters and a cannon shell from an Me 109 punched a hole in the perspex of my turret and the same burst put a few holes in the aircraft fuselage. The main damage was done to the Elsan [a portable toilet located aft of the bomb-bay, on the port side.] There was a big hole blown in the bottom. A messy business. The icy wind whistling through my damaged turret was more than somewhat uncomfortable. However, I was too scared to worry as I kept searching the sky. Every now and then we would see signs of tracer flying through the air and sometimes there would be an explosion and a big ball of flame would tumble earthwards.

'All in all, it was a fairly shaky old do.'

Another Australian mid-upper gunner, Warrant Officer Alan Strickland, was to experience only a routine run over the target with his Pathfinder crew in Lancaster R-ROGER, from No. 83 Squadron, Wyton.

'On this occasion,' he said, 'our duties over the target were to be special blind markers. We had a good run in and dropped on radar, checking visually. Some of the first wave of Main Force had already arrived and were bombing the preliminary markers. We dropped at zero minus one and the first markers were dropped at zero minus five. I estimate that general bombing commenced at zero minus two. This distracted attention from us and our run in was simple. We dropped a double colour (reds and yellows, as I recall) and as ours were the only double colours on the target-marking for the attack they could be readily identified. Having dropped, we observed sticks of bombs falling across our markers which were well backed up by other Pathfinder aircraft.

'Over the target, flak was not particularly heavy and I estimate there were only some forty heavy guns. However, searchlights co-operated with fighters and caused some losses in this area.'

Pilot Officer Paddy Gundelach, Australian Lancaster pilot of No. 460 Squadron, Binbrook, made only passing reference to the target:

'I saw many small fires on the ground, especially after leaving the target area. These, we presumed, were our bombers burning after having been shot down. "Mac" McFarlane logged their positions.'

After diving and successfully blowing out the fire in his port outer engine and evading further fighter attack by violent corkscrewing, Flight Lieutenant Dan Conway, RAAF, of No. 467 Squadron, Waddington, found himself at 17 500 feet instead of 21 500 and setting the course for the target which his navigator, Joe Wesley, had given him.

'It took a lot longer to reach the target than its nearness indicated,' said Conway. 'I think that it was about this time that the airspeed indicator began to play up. We had been plagued with icing trouble at the pitot head and on several previous occasions had flown to and from the target with no indicated airspeed. This trouble seemed to occur when flying in mist or vapour trails at altitude and we were now in a slight haze. Fortunately, the target was quiet when we arrived, with few searchlights. The raid had been scattered and we had trouble locating our target-indicators through the smoke. Found the TIs after some exploration and did a good run at 16 500 feet. Seemed to have the whole place to ourselves at this stage which we didn't regard as a good thing. Having brought our bombs so far and having lost so many of our mates we didn't intend to waste them. Set course for home on three motors and with airspeed indicator definitely unserviceable. This handicapped the navigator as I couldn't give him an airspeed. I therefore asked the wireless operator to obtain a fix. He reported that his set was unserviceable. He suspected the generator operating from the damaged motor.'

But at least Conway and his crew were on their way home.

Conway's navigator, Sergeant Joseph Wesley, was reconciled to the fact that they would be late on target after the Ju 88's cannon shells had hit and stopped the port outer motor.

'With the three sound engines we resumed course for the target area which we could now see well lit up,' he recalled, 'and although we were about twenty minutes overdue on our scheduled time for bombing, quite a few of the bomber force were still backing up the markers and our bombs were dispatched on them on our correct heading.'

Pilot Officer Ray Curling, RAAF, pilot of Lancaster A-ABLE, of Mildenhall's No. 622 Squadron, was not to cross the target unchallenged:

'By the time we bombed at 0125 at 20 000 feet we had about six- to seven-tenths of cloud cover,' he reported. 'It was a hot target with huge fires burning below. On our bombing run an Fw 190 attacked us. It closed to 400 yards. Our rear gunner fired a three-second burst which appeared to hit the fighter which dived away and was not seen again. We got our bombs away and turned for home. By this time we had seen a total of approximately twenty of our own aircraft going down. We were feeling more scared that night than on the previous trip to Berlin.'

Flight Sergeant Walter Morrisby, from the rear turret of Lancaster EA-U of No. 49 Squadron, Fiskerton, in No. 5 Group, had a brief but vivid recollection of the bomb run:

'The whole of our bombing run was between fighter flares and the entire area was extremely bright . . . on the run in, flak was heavy but not as heavy as one would expect. Searchlights were numerous although most aircraft that I saw coned over the target area appeared to be shot down by fighters, not flak. During the entire operation we had not suffered any damage by flak nor attacks by fighters. Two Fw 190 fighters were observed just after "bombs gone", the first appearing below our aircraft heading in the opposite direction and the second, travelling from port to starboard, about a thousand feet below our own height.'

The sightings did not result in combat over the target for Morrisby's crew.

It was a different view of the target area from the navigator's seat of Flying Officer Harold Barker, DFC, RAAF, in the cockpit of the Mosquito Mark IV v-victor, of No. 139 Squadron, Upwood, the Pathfinder Force base in Huntingdonshire.

With his pilot, Flying Officer Allan Brown, RAF, Barker had been briefed to drop four 500-pound general-purpose bombs on target-indicator markers dropped by other PFF Mosquitoes ahead of the Main Force bomber stream. After bombing, they were to orbit the target and assess results.

'We arrived over the target on time after following a devious route and large fires were soon evident,' said Barker.

'We bombed from 25 000 feet. A layer of cloud approximately 5000 feet below us veiled the target area. It was thin stratus cloud, though, and the markers and fires could be seen through it. However, it acted as a huge reflector and the Lancasters were easily seen as they made their bombing runs and continued on. We stayed in the target area for about half an hour and observed dozens of combats between fighters and Lancasters. There were many explosions in the air as the Lancs blew up. We could see many German fighters around us and below, making their attacks on the lower flying Lancs but we were not attacked as there were too many easier targets to be seen.'

One of the Lancasters to be shot down before reaching the target was V-VICTOR, of No. 166 Squadron, Kirmington, in No. 1 Group.

When the Constantinople-born British wireless air gunner Flight Sergeant Sidney Whitlock jolted down on snow-covered German ground, he had found the frozen earth too hard to dig a hole in which to bury his parachute—an evader's first move. He carried the tangled canopy in his arms until he came to a ditch where he dumped it hoping that it would not be noticed for some time because of falling snow.

'I had left the fields where I had landed, to try and get my bearings as the navigator had had no time to carry out our long-prepared plan of letting us know where we were in case of having to bale out. Before I had gone more than a short distance I was surrounded by armed German civilians with snarling dogs on leashes.'

No coded signal confirming that the target had been attacked would be sent back from over Nuremberg that night by Whitlock.

From his mid-upper turret in Halifax D-DOG of No. 640 Squadron, Leconfield, in No. 4 Group, Flight Sergeant Harry Webb—'Spider' to his crew—had helped fight off five German fighter attacks in the last thirty minutes before commencing the run in to the target. Watching and waiting, far from his home in Hinkley, Leicestershire, Harry Webb was prepared for the worst as the bomb-doors opened. Strangely, nothing happened.

'We bombed the main target,' he reported briefly. 'Later, the camera photos showed that the bombs had been bang on the TIs.'

Despite the dash and determination of the German defences, the brilliance of the moon and the treachery of the March winds, the bombers were getting through.

It was flak and searchlights, not fighters, that struck at Lancaster z-zebra, of No. 166 Squadron, Kirmington, as its pilot, Pilot Officer Bridges, lined up for the bombing run.

Flight Sergeant Sidney Lipman, the young RAF flight engineer who had been so keen to fly that night even as a relieving 'spare bod' crew member, could see many fires on the ground as the pilot beside him held z-zebra on a steady bombing-run course.

Steadily approaching the target, bomb doors open, the Lancaster's heading was directed by the bomb aimer until he finally pressed the bomb release with the 'Mickey Mouse' electrical release gear clicking around as the load left the bays in planned sequence.

'The bomb-doors shut and then we got caught by searchlights,' said Lipman. 'The ack-ack came all around us. The searchlights blinded us. We climbed and then came down, very sharply. The searchlights missed us and caught another aircraft and the flak brought him down. Coming out of the target area we caught sight of enemy aircraft but they did not see us.'

Pitted with shrapnel, Lipman's Lancaster was, so far, safely on its way home to Kirmington.

For Pilot Officer John Goldsmith, the Canadian navigator from Halifax, Nova Scotia, and the crew of Lancaster CF-S, of No. 625 Squadron, Kelstern, in No. 1 Group, the problem was not flak or searchlights, as his diary entry indicates: 'Flak moderate. Searchlights not very effective. Bombing appeared to be scattered . . .'

Although this was the Canadian's thirteenth operational trip with No. 625 Squadron, his luck was in.

'An aircraft almost ran into us on the bombing run. We were not sure what type it was but believed it to be an Me 210. If we were correct in our assumption this would give an idea of the large number of aircraft used that night by the Germans since the Me 210 had been taken out of production in 1942 and I don't believe its successor, the Me 410, became operational until the summer of 1944.'

The Australian barrister and solicitor turned navigator, Flying Officer Sydney Johnson, was one of two specialist navigators aboard Lancaster x-xray, of No. 156 Squadron based at Warboys in the Pathfinder Force's No. 8 Group. Johnson's only reference to entering or leaving the target area was in the 'remarks' section of his navigator's log book, referring to his crew's role in PFF's activities over the target: 'Primary blind-marker—duty carried out.'

Flying Officer Robert McHattie, the former Scottish police-man from Banffshire, now the captain of a special-duties 'Airborne Cigar' Lancaster e-easy of No. 101 Squadron, Ludford Magna, having evaded a salvo of air-to-air rockets from a Ju 88 and watched a Lancaster corkscrewing down past his nose, followed by a diving Me 110, found that the attack had not long begun when he arrived over Nuremberg.

'The searchlights and anti-aircraft fire seemed only moderate to me,' he said. 'The target was well marked and numerous fires had already broken out. We had a smooth, uninterrupted bombing run and we got the bombs away first run and turned for home. For a short distance before reaching the target contrailing at 21 000 feet had become intermittent but almost as soon as we left the target a pretty solid contrail appeared in front of me—same height, same track. Reasoning that this might afford a measure of cover in the bright moonlight and that one contrail would be less easily seen than two I entered it and flew along it for about fifty miles.'

Having witnessed the criss-cross tracer of many combats and evaded an air-to-air rocket attack, McHattie's crew were glad to see the target.

Among them was the wireless air gunner, Sergeant John

Allison, who noted that '. . . despite the defences through which we lost ninety-seven bombers, one of Bomber Command's worst nights of the war, the attack was a success and we left the target blazing.'

The target area recollections of Pilot Officer Bowman, RAAF, captain of the crew of Lancaster J-JIG of No. 463 Squadron, Waddington, were typical of the night, particularly for pilots busy with the bombing run.

'I do not remember too much about the actual target area except that it was very hot with plenty of fighters, searchlights and flak. The place seemed one mass of flames with explosions going off everywhere. There were many aircraft shot down over the target area as the flak seemed accurate and some were hit by the fighters. We were very pleased when the bombs left the aircraft and we got out of the area as quick as we could and set course for home.'

On the way into the target from as far back as the enemy coast on the English Channel, Sergeant George Dykes, the Canadian from Saskatoon, Saskatchewan, had seen no enemy aircraft from the rear turret of his Halifax Mark III, Q-QUEEN, of No. 433 Squadron, Skipton-on-Swale, Yorkshire. Nor in fact had he seen very many RAF aircraft of the bomber stream.

'We were evidently a couple of minutes late getting to the target,' said Dykes, 'and no target-indicators were visible when we arrived. However, in spite of quite a lot of cloud the fires could easily be seen and I believe our bomb aimer, George Wade, bombed on these fires.

'Immediately after the "bombs gone" call I spotted a twin-engined aircraft astern, to starboard and slightly below us. I called for evasive action and opened fire together with the mid-upper gunner, Douglas Carruthers, another Canadian. The enemy fighter evidently had two 20-millimetre cannon. He broke off his attack quite close to us but got no hits on us. He went right through our .303 machine-gun fire, from both turrets, and disappeared to port. We had just straightened away for home again when the same type of fighter was seen to be coming at us from a starboard bow, below, position. On this pass he put several shots into our starboard outer engine which immediately quit. The pilot, Ronald Reinelt, and the flight engineer, Peppercorn, were unable to feather the dead prop and the aircraft became very difficult to control.

'At the same time fire broke out in one of the wing tanks beside the windmilling prop of the dead starboard outer motor. I believe our flight engineer switched the other three motors onto the burning tank and after about thirty minutes the fire burned itself out.

'The fighter may have been hit by our return fire on his second pass as he did not return to the attack although we were very vulnerable and could not take any further evasive action due to the drag of the still-windmilling starboard outer prop.'

Flight Lieutenant Robin Knights, DFC, another No. 101 Squadron pilot on Airborne Cigar special duties was among the aircraft destined to wait, milling around over the assumed target on ETA. He was not impressed with the results of the attack as he saw it from his Lancaster D-DOG, Serial No. LL 773:

'It was nothing like the size of conflagration normally seen on these occasions but there was enough light to see other aircraft when running over the target. They were coming in all directions, from dead ahead and at angles from both bows and quarters. Some were above and some below. Those above were the most unhealthy as with their bomb doors yawning open, and bombs falling away, the danger of being hit was very great. Several times I took violent evasive action both to avoid being bombed from above and also to avoid aircraft coming in the opposite direction. It was an absolute free-for-all mêlée and the bombing run was hardly straight and level. The bomb aimer (Sergeant Morgan) claimed to have seen a coloured flare so there may have been a Pathfinder to start if off. I personally think that a very large percentage of the losses were collisions as I had so many near misses in a comparatively short period.'

Pilot Officer Ern Mustard, of No. 463 (RAAF) Squadron, Waddington, flying his veteran Lancaster finishing-school aircraft with its reduced bomb load, was to enter and leave the target with no particular memories that he could later recall.

For Sergeant David Davidson, flight engineer of Halifax EY-A of No. 78 Squadron, Breighton, in No. 4 Group, the target came into sight at 0018. Transition of it was to be memorable.

'Very bright over target,' Davidson recalled. 'I can make out the shapes of some streets with the fires and explosions. Here and there a few Lancs and Halifaxes in sight. Bombs away 0123 and we start turning off to starboard. Height: 20 500 feet. Air temp.: – 32° Centigrade. See a Halifax going down in vertical dive towards target at 0124 with three Ju 88s on its tail. Smoke or haze over parts of target area. The Halifax is diving head-first for this. We turn to starboard and completely lose sight of diving Halifax and Ju 88 fighters. On course for French coast and holding to 20 000 feet at 0126. Lancaster, going in opposite direction, goes over the top of us, very close. Too close! A bit of nattering on inter-com. We were late on target but that Lanc. is even later, heading for the target at this time of morning, 0130. Christ! There's the target coming up again, in front. Quick call to the navigator to check the "off target" course. The skipper goes to set the checked course on the gyro compass and finds what's happened: the gyro had toppled on our first turn away from the target. That Lancaster was on its way home when he passed over the top of us!'

For Flying Officer Ronald Rudd, RCAF, the navigator in Halifax R-ROGER of No. 429 Squadron, Leeming, in York-shire, his time spent over the target was remarkable only for its quietness and total lack of drama. More than flak or fighters it was the moon that Rudd recalled: 'It was a bril-liant moonlit night,' he said.

'I believe we were high that night and I remember the lane of flares outlining the target area. There seemed to be a definite pattern of flares outlining the run in as well as the run from the target. There was not a great deal of flak and evidence of fighter activity. I am not certain about flak but it seems to stick in my mind that this was one trip where things were very smooth over the target. As I remember, our bombing run was uneventful.'

Flying over the target with Rudd, a student from Owen Sound, Ontario, were: Warrant Officer 2, M. A. Fernandez, a Guatamala-born American in the RCAF, pilot; Flight Sergeant L. M. Shetler, RCAF, bomb aimer; Sergeant M. Stewart, RCAF, flight engineer; Sergeant Dawson, RAF, wireless air gunner; Sergeant R. Christie, RCAF, mid-upper gunner; Sergeant K. Baker, RAF, rear gunner.

Flight Sergeant Reginald Parissien, Kentish-born flight engineer of No. 156 Squadron's Lancaster GT-C, one of the Pathfinder aircraft marking the target for the bomber stream, had seen two aircraft going down in flames so he was more than usually alert as his pilot, Warrant Officer Higgs, headed the Lancaster in towards Nuremberg.

'The target area was sustaining a heavy attack when we reached it,' said Parissien. 'Having unloaded we proceeded homeward.'

'Proceeded homeward' was putting it rather mildly.

Flying Officer William Barclay, RAAF, navigating Lancaster F-FOX, another No. 156 Squadron aircraft from the PFF base at Upwood, dealt briskly with the target as he logged the details:

'Bombs were dropped at 0104.4 (our time on target was 0105 compared with normal zero hour of 0110). Bombing on green markers and H2S checking. Flak over target was light.'

Long before the target came into view, Flight Sergeant Leonard Pratt, flight engineer of No. 427 Squadron's Halifax V-VICTOR, had been concerned about fuel consumption on this deep penetration attack.

'We got onto the two largest main tanks at some distance from the target area giving sufficient fuel to get us well out of trouble before having to change again,' he said. 'The overload was pumped over as soon as possible and was complete before we reached the target area.'

Of Nuremberg itself, Pratt said, 'We reached the target and I remember thinking how miserable it looked. It was partially covered by cloud and there didn't seem to be many markers. The Master Bomber called for "backers up" and we were directed to bomb a differently coloured marker to that specified at the briefing. I think, in fact, it was the greens. There wasn't much flak over the target area. Our bombing run was reasonably successful as far as I know and we got the bomb load away without too much trouble.'

In still another Lancaster of the Pathfinder Force, v-VICTOR, Serial No. JB 344, of 'B' Flight, No. 405 Squadron (RCAF), Gransden Lodge, Flight Lieutenant Reuben William Wright, DFM, was lining up Nuremberg in the bomb-sight of his bomb aimer's position in the nose of the aircraft.

For Wright, a Canadian, this was to be the forty-eighth target out of a total of sixty-two operational trips.

It was an experienced crew: Flight Lieutenant J. R. McDonald, DFC, RAF, pilot (later promoted to Squadron Leader and awarded the DSO); Pilot Officer G. G. Bellamy, DFM, RAF, navigator, (later awarded the DFC); Flight Lieutenant E. R. Wright, RAF, flight engineer, (later awarded the DFC); Flying Officer J. C. Gibbs, RCAF, wireless air gunner, (later awarded the DFC); Flight Lieutenant T. R. N. Duff, DFC, RCAF, mid-upper gunner; Flying Officer J. D. Routledge, RCAF, rear gunner, (later awarded a DFC).

Wright found the target covered by heavy overcast with moonlight above the cloud. No fighters had been seen on the way in to the target. The bomb load he was about to drop consisted of one 4000-pound 'blockbuster' bomb, five 1000-pound bombs, one 500-pound bomb and four hooded Pathfinder flares.

'The flares and target-indicators were fairly widespread,' said Wright, 'and I believe the bombs were rather dispersed —whether on the target or not I do not know.'

Sergeant Frederick Shaw, the Canadian rear gunner of Lancaster w-WILLIAM from No. 12 Squadron, Wickenby, Lincolnshire, was lucky even to have reached Nuremberg after the series of fighter attacks that were made on his aircraft within thirty minutes of the target.

Temporarily blinded by a cannon shell from a Junkers

Ju 88 coming in to attack from dead astern, he had both eyes blackened and cannon shell fragments embedded in his left eye. With the Lancaster taking such violent evasive action that he was not sure whether or not it was out of control and with the intercom, oxygen and hydraulic systems to his turret cut off, Shaw was to retain little recollection of entering the target area.

Fortunately his turret had been facing dead astern when the hydraulic system was shot up so he was able to open the turret doors and grope his way up the fuselage to get his parachute pack from its stowage. He was unable to find it: a shell from the fighter had blown it from its position.

'At this time the mid-upper gunner got out of his turret and came over to see what had happened to me. He shouted in my ear that the aircraft was now under control and that he would find my 'chute and let me know when it became necessary to bail out. The skipper in the meantime had feathered the prop and we dropped our bomb load at a low level.'

So far it had been a comparatively quiet trip for Flight Sergeant William Stenning, wireless air gunner in Halifax MH-L, of No. 51 Squadron, Snaith, flown by the American RCAF pilot, Flight Lieutenant J. Pawell.

'It seemed no time and we were approaching the target,' he reported. 'Bob, the bomb aimer, reported sighting the target and we went onto Master Bomber frequency. The area was well alight and I recall seeing the pattern of streets and roads. Joe Pawell, the skipper, had a cine camera going. He'd also used this on a trip to Schweinfurt but I never saw the films. We were soon going in and back down. I went to the flare chute and plugged into the intercom to listen to the bomb aimer. Bombs were away, and the photo-flash bomb, and we were away too, turning to starboard and losing height in a dive. I went back to my position in the nose and looking out saw a Lancaster diving steeply followed by what looked like an Me 110. The Lancaster caught fire.'

In another No. 4 Group Halifax, LK-E of No. 578 Squadron, the navigator, Pilot Officer John Lambert, from

Newcastle on Tyne, was about to fly into a target area for the last time.

Approaching the run in to Nuremberg, and in accordance with the crew drill, Lambert folded up his navigational gear as he sat directly over the forward escape hatch. Over the target, navigation was from notes on his knee-pad taken from callings by the bomb aimer, Pilot Officer Crate, RCAF.

'I think we had the bomb-doors open when there was a shout from the rear gunner,' Lambert said. 'His sentence was unfinished as the aircraft shuddered from a rain of cannon shells and the intercom was destroyed. The aircraft was on fire and being thrown around the sky by the pilot, Pilot Officer Barton. A signal over the emergency light flashers was misunderstood by the forward crew (navigator, wireless air gunner and bomb aimer) and I donned my parachute pack. In removing the escape hatch door which had jammed I caught the rip-cord inadvertently on some part of the aircraft interior. The parachute opened in the aircraft and in a flash it was sucked out of the half-open hatch and I was whipped out after it. I was amazed to find myself dangling in mid-air with a torn parachute canopy flapping above me. It was still moonlight but all seemed very quiet and there was no sign of the target. It was bitterly cold. My hands were unprotected and I must have been ejected from the aircraft at a considerable height. Because of the damaged parachute canopy I descended rapidly and hit the middle of a very hard, frozen field.'

Pilot Officer Lambert's career as a navigator was over.

In still another Halifax, N-NAN of No. 433 Squadron, Skipton Bridge, Yorkshire, in No. 6 Group, the Canadian rear gunner, Pilot Officer John McLauchlan, and his crew were making the last bombing run of a tour of thirty trips. On landing back in Yorkshire they would be screened from operations.

McLauchlan remembers that his pilot, Pilot Officer Chris Nielsen, and the bomb aimer, Warrant Officer Les Milward, a Canadian from Moosomin, Saskatchewan, were making the bomb run when the second pilot, flying his indoctrination trip before initiating his own crew, reported that there was a fire in the starboard inner motor.

'Didn't I know it,' said McLauchlan. 'The flames were streaming aft and licking at my turret. I was getting burned. I heard Chris, our pilot, tell the second dickie to feather the prop on the starboard inner. The next thing I knew we were in a spin and heading down fast. I reached for my parachute in between being either pinned down or thrown from side to side of my turret. I couldn't get the bloody pack clipped onto my harness. I was all thumbs and still being thrown about and being burned. Rather than stay there and be roasted I decided to bail out. One last try and then something caught. I'd practised this many times before but never in a spin. I pulled the rip-cord handle and was immediately plucked out of the aircraft. I had not pulled out the connections for my oxygen mask or the heater cords for my gloves and shoes and so smashed my head against the aircraft. Down I went, though, covered in blood. I could see the bombs dropping on Nuremberg and the flak rushing up. I landed beside a church on the outskirts of Nuremberg. I remember thinking how close I had come to being spiked by the spire. People came running. Six or seven of them grabbed me and began all tugging in different directions. Eventually we got all sorted out. I was placed in a school for Hitler Jugend and my wounds were tended by a lady of the area.'

Pilot Officer Samuel Moorhouse, flying his twenty-third operational trip with No. 460 (RAAF) Squadron, Binbrook, recalled only that the bombs of his crew's Lancaster were dropped on a due south heading.

To Pilot Officer Harry Mackinnon, RAFVR, the navigator of Lancaster N-NAN of No. 57 Squadron, East Kirby, Nuremberg was a target memorable for the fact that never had time passed so slowly for him.

After having energetically corkscrewed his Lancaster S-SUGAR into the target area, Wing Commander S. P. Daniels, DFC and bar, commanding officer in No. 35 Squadron in the Pathfinder Force, found a lot of cloud over Nuremberg. 'We did not consider the raid very successful,' was his comment.

Over the target, Pilot Officer Donald Richardson, RAF, navigating Lancaster VN-F of No. 50 Squadron, Skellingthorpe, in No. 5 Group, found that the actual winds indicated that his pilot, Pilot Officer Lloyd, would have to steer 150° for nine minutes. Richardson's aircraft was not fitted with H2S and he had had to rely on forecast and broadcast winds, which had been in error and the cause of poor tracking over Germany.

'About thirty miles accumulated error in wind from the last Gee-fix took us about seven and a half minutes to fly to the target,' he said. 'Errors from this cause were larger than on other raids.'

Sergeant Eric Morrey, flight engineer in Lancaster JO-B, of No. 463 (RAAF) Squadron, remembered that the crew's bomb aimer, Flight Sergeant Tom Morris, RAAF, got the bombs away on the first bombing run. As the bombs went, the aircraft lifted slightly and began to climb to 21 000 feet.

'Vic Brill, our navigator, soon gave us our new course for home,' said Morrey, 'and Charlie Cassell, the pilot, was getting a bit more speed out of the Lanc . . . the flak was considerably heavier now and our aircraft was buffeted about to some extent.'

Sergeant James Maclean, rear-gunner of Lancaster F-FOX, No. 9 Squadron, Bardney, after an uneventful trip to Nuremberg, reported that flak was active in defence of the target but he did not observe any fighters. Leaving the target in good visibility Maclean was glad to hear the Canadian navigator, Flying Officer Logan, giving the first of the homeward courses to the pilot, Flight Lieutenant Pearce.

Sergeant Geoffrey Jennings, formerly a capstan operator at Maidenhead, Berkshire, but now the mid-upper gunner of Lancaster G-GEORGE, of No. 630 Squadron, East Kirkby, recalled that the enemy activity over Nuremberg and immediately afterwards was probably more intense than any he had experienced previously. 'It was obvious at the time that the enemy was either waiting or had reached the area very quickly when our objective became obvious.'

The Canadian rear gunner, Flight Sergeant Roger Callaway, from Alberta, who had volunteered to fly a 'spare bod' trip with Flight Lieutenant Shedd in Lancaster OW-N, of No. 426 Squadron, Linton-on-Ouse, in No. 6 Group, retained a clear recollection of the target area: '. . . things were fairly quiet until Nuremberg when all hell broke loose. Although we were not attacked I witnessed many aircraft going down and Jerry seemed all around us and it was sure cold . . .'

The former policeman, Pilot Officer Frank Collis, of No. 207 Squadron, Spilsby, in No. 5 Group, still ahead of the first wave of bombers, arrived punctually at Nuremberg: 'At 0110 we bombed from 21 000 feet on a heading of 170° Magnetic.'

To have bombed accurately and on time to the second at the briefed zero hour of 0110 was something of an achievement on this wild and confused night.

Despite bright moonlight and the presence of enemy fighters observed from the bomber, Lancaster u-uncle of No. 3 Group's No. 622 Squadron, Mildenhall, reached the target area safely but the navigator, Sergeant Edgar Hazelwood, recorded no impressions of conditions of the target. He was content just to get there and get out again.

Squadron Leader Arthur Doubleday, DFC, who flew Lancaster x-xray of No. 467 (RAAF) Squadron, Waddington, said that he was not sure but it was not his recollection that the Pathfinder Force had been late with their marking of the target at Nuremberg.

For Doubleday, the target was memorable as the occasion when ' . . . Bill Brill was in strife over the target as a couple of belts of ammunition, out of an aircraft which blew up in front of him, hit his outer starboard engine.'

As the harassed Lancasters and Halifaxes weaved, corkscrewed or just dived their way out of the confused and embattled target area above Nuremberg and the valley of the Pegnitz one thing was paramountly clear—it was a night that had shaken many even experienced bomber crews of the RAF. Truly, it had been a bad night at Nuremberg.

5   The Way Out

If only for the reason that it had been a long night, bitter with a cold that froze and jammed the moving parts of over-lubricated machine guns, the British crews were glad to be heading home from Nuremberg. Particularly the air gunners, cramped behind the .303 Brownings banked in their turrets, desperately trying to stay awake, if not alert, during uneventful but uneasy stages of the deep penetration flight over enemy territory, or suddenly striving to achieve instant, accurate deflection shooting while being flung violently around the sky as their aircraft corkscrewed to stay safely out of the glowing gun-sights of attacking fighters.

It had been a long haul, too, for the pilots, captains without second pilots or dual controls, flying alone from the left-hand seats of their Halifaxes or Lancasters. (The second pilots, flying in some of the Halifaxes and Lancasters for operational 'blooding' were often regarded by their host crews as being more a source of irritation in the crowded cockpits than as potential take-over skippers in the event of an emergency.)

For the navigators, coping with the escalating complications set in train early in the night by the perverse behaviour of the forecast winds, it had been hour after anxious hour of calculation and re-calculation, checking and re-checking, over-shadowed always by thoughts of the chances of committing the ultimate, humiliating navigational sin of not being able to answer, confidently and immediately, the inevitable plaintive question from the cockpit, 'Where are we, navigator?'

114

The wireless air gunners had had a night of divided loyalties, of time shared between monitoring the dials and the knurled knobs of their radio equipment and an anxious, eyeball-by-eyeball sky-watch in support of the searching gunners.

For the flight engineers it had been a night, primarily, of remembering to conserve as much fuel as possible on this deep penetration operation so that on return the occurrence of fog at base and the consequent need for diversion to the nearest airfield still open would not end in disaster with fuel-starved motors one by one spluttering and back-firing into heart-stopping silence.

For many of the bomb aimers, lying prone at their bomb sights, the night had been one of frustration and anxiety, culminating in a time of confusion and uncertainty, as they circled with bomb-doors open above the cascading flares and scattered ground fires of the elusive target-area aiming point.

Few if any of the Main Force Halifaxes and Lancasters had spent less than seven hours in the air from bomb-pregnant, fuel-burdened take-off to a frankly thankful touch-down back in England. (In effect they had all flown, non-stop, the equivalent in time of a Boeing 707 trans-Atlantic flight from Heathrow to Kennedy and back again, with much of it in aggressively defended enemy air space.)

To be standing on English earth again—or even on oil-rainbowed English tarmac—as a cool, clear dawn began to drive off the night of 30 March, a night already retreating into history, was to be amazed that it had all actually happened and yet here one was, incredibly but undoubtedly still alive. As much alive as the pair of blackbirds skittering noisily in the hedgerow beyond the bomb dump; as much alive as the yawning, gum-booted farmer whistling up his dog from the furrows of the turnip field beyond the parked and chocked aircraft which once more had safely brought one home again.

This was the time when young men not normally given to sentiment would mutter 'She's a good old bitch' and give the matt black fuselage a friendly thump as they would the shoulder of a tried and trusted friend.

Crew transport driven by WAAFs would arrive then and there would be much yawning and stretching as the men picked up helmets, Mae Wests, gloves, parachute harnesses and packs, navigation satchels, charts, logs, coffee flasks, computers, dropped pencils and clip-boards of classified signals and navigation information. There was, at this point, a tendency to move and walk in a slowed down, slightly disorientated kind of way like mourners after a burial.

Strangely, now that it was all over, there was little of the animated chaffing and joking and horse-play that sometimes relieved the tension prior to an operational take-off. The conversation now was tired and superficially concerned mainly with apparent trivia:

'Aren't we due for leave soon?'

'I've left my bloody helmet in the aircraft.'

'Did anybody stoke up the stove before we left?'

'Christ, don't you ever buy any cigarettes of your own?'

'This WAAF driver will kill us yet.'

'Who's got the laundry tickets?'

'What time does that bus leave for Lincoln?'

'She said she'd be there at opening-time.'

Occasionally these and other inconsequential exchanges, conversational clutchings at the safe straws of normal every-day life, would be interpolated with direct references to the so-recently shared experiences of the diminishing night:

'Jesus, I was cold coming home.'

'Sorry about the landing, chaps.'

'That port outer motor sounds a bit sick.'

'I wasn't going around again for quids.'

'Did you see the wing come off that Halifax?'

'Bloody hell, I could sleep for a week.'

'One thing about the Ruhr—at least it's quicker.'

'I only counted two parachutes.'

'I thought that Lanc. was going to carve us in half.'

'The dumb bastards never even saw us.'

'Some of these clots must start weaving on take-off.'

Generally, though, there seemed to be, by unspoken agreement and tacit understanding, a tendency to forget about the whole bloody business at least until they'd had a drink.

A WAAF driving a tractor tows an 8000-lb blockbuster bomb to the waiting bomb-bays of a Lancaster.   *Air Ministry*

In this photograph of a Bomber Command Lancaster, the war-time censor appears to have eliminated squadron code-letters, manufacturer's serial number and details of armament in front, mid-upper and rear turrets. *Air Ministry*

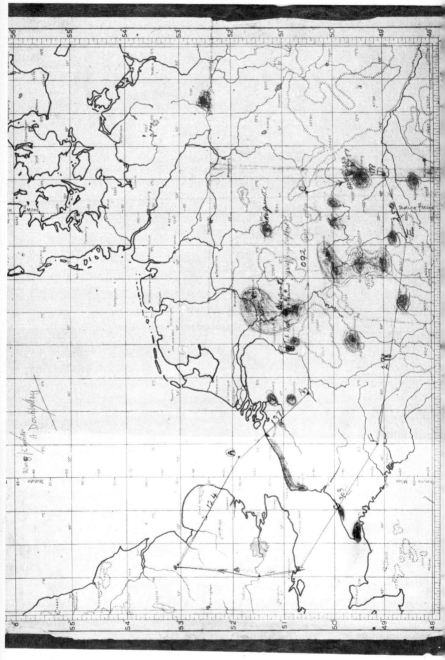

Nuremberg route plan, with flak areas indicated, prepared by Pilot Officer
D. S. Richardson, No. 50 Squadron, Skellingthorpe, Lincolnshire.
D. S. Richardson

To each and every crew, the night had been an individual experience.

Despite a reduced airspeed due to the loss of the port outer motor during the bombing run, Squadron Leader Bill Brill, of No. 463 (RAAF) Squadron, had an uneventful but unpleasant trip home, lagging behind the bomber stream.

'It was most nerve-wracking,' the customarily unflappable Brill said. 'The German fighters relished stragglers and they could take full advantage of ground radar to effect interceptions. However, it seemed that the fighter force had spent itself during the earlier holocaust and we were unmolested. Our main problem was to keep on track and stay clear of the defended areas. Still, being last had its advantages because the earlier aircraft who were a little off course pin-pointed the defended areas.

'We finally landed back at base over an hour after the main group, probably more than normally exhausted.

'One other aircraft from our squadron landed long after the remainder and strangely enough it carried my younger brother as navigator. The squadron commander was quite convinced that he had lost both Brills that night.'

An inspection of Squadron Leader Brill's Lancaster, JO-K, revealed that the cause of the port outer motor failure was the fouling of fuel lines and other controls to the engine. These lay just under the leading edge of the mainplane and twenty or thirty rounds of belted British .303 ammunition were found lodged in the leading edge of the mainplace between the two port motors.

'Quite obviously,' said Brill, 'the explosion immediately in front of us as we ran into the target was no less than one of our aircraft disintegrating. How we missed being struck by heavier and larger pieces of it is little short of a miracle. However the wireless operator who was standing in the astrodome position said later that a Merlin engine missed us by inches.

'So much for a raid which almost decimated Bomber Command and yet achieved so little.'

Squadron Leader Brill's flying time to Nuremberg and back: 8.35 hours.

Subsequently, he was to comment: 'In retrospect I can say that this trip was the most frightening and perhaps the most frustrating of all those in which I was directly involved. We lost almost a hundred aircraft with the loss of six or seven hundred highly trained young men and as far as I could gather we scattered bombs over half of Germany. The loss of men represented up to a thousand man-years of highly specialized and most expensive training.'

Having had to fight their way into the target and out again, the crew of Flight Sergeant Hayes' Lancaster VN-N of No. 50 Squadron were more than usually glad to be back, safe and sound, at Skellingthorpe. For the Australian mid-upper gunner, after a long, anxious night in his turret, the relief was enormous.

'On return to base we were all physically exhausted yet curiously exhilarated,' he said. 'We examined the aircraft for damage but there was surprisingly little. There was a great buzz of talk at de-briefing, much excited chatter in the huts and a long period of sleeplessness for most of us for the remainder of that night. The squadron was stood down next day and we were all sent off on leave.'

Within minutes of helping to hit and set on fire the Ju 88 which had attacked his Halifax ZA-L over the target, Flying Officer Gerry Girardau was glad to hear that his pilot, Warrant Officer Paddy Clarke, was back on the homeward course.

On the way out of Germany there were a number of occasions when Girardau, from his rear turret, saw other aircraft being attacked although the cloud had built up as had been expected some hours earlier. But neither he nor the Canadian mid-upper gunner, Pilot Officer Don Johnson, had to use their guns again that night.

'Our aeroplane was third to land at base where we received a hearty welcome from the ground crew. De-briefing was carried out and we explained how Met. had boobed for the trip to the target. After some hours' sleep and return to the flights we learned that six out of our squadron's twelve aircraft had failed to return.'

Nuremberg had certainly been a bad night for No. 10 Squadron, RAF Station, Melbourne, Yorkshire.

'It was a big shock to learn that over all ninety-four aeroplanes had been reported missing,' said Girardau. 'My own view of this great loss was that it was due to cloud missing on the half-moon trip and the Germans must have known about the operation as we took off.'

Girardau had spent 7.55 hours airborne in the rear turret of his Halifax.

Another Australian air gunner in No. 10 Squadron, Flying Officer Fred Stuart, in the mid-upper turret of Halifax ZA-M, flew home to Yorkshire with the freezing slip-stream howling through the hole punched in his turret perspex by a cannon shell from an Me 109 over the target.

'On return to base we were not very happy to hear 'Milkpail', the call sign for our base, warning us that there were 'Bandits', or German intruder aircraft, in the area and that we were to disperse. However we were shortly afterwards recalled and, thank goodness, were able to land at our home base.

'. . . The horror of it hit home next day when we heard the emotionless voice of a BBC news-reader announcing that Bomber Command RAF had raided the German city of Nuremberg and that ninety-eight of our aircraft were missing over Europe. How many over the North Sea? How many over England? How many killed and wounded in the aircraft which had returned "safely" to base?'

For Warrant Officer Alan Strickland, RAAF, of No. 83 Squadron, another mid-upper gunner, it was a tiring trip home with head-winds slowing his Pathfinder Lancaster which still had to run the gauntlet of enemy fighters near the French coast on the way out.

'On reaching England we found a number of bases closed because of fog,' he recalled. 'As we were now short of fuel we landed at Downham Market instead of Wyton. I had considered this night to have been a fighter night and had estimated our losses to be between thirty and forty aircraft.

I was indeed surprised to discover that our losses were about ninety-seven.'

After having been airborne for 7.20 hours, Pilot Officer Paddy Gaudelach of No. 460 (RAAF) Squadron landed his Lancaster M-MIKE thankfully back at Binbrook.

'Having consumed my rum ration and been de-briefed I slept for some hours,' said Gundelach. 'On waking, a solemn-faced steward said, "I'm glad to see you back. Ninety-four of our aircraft did not return." I wondered how many of my friends and acquaintances were among those missing. I then did a quick mental calculation—two trips behind me and twenty-eight to go to complete my tour. I did not go back to sleep again.'

Like No. 463 Squadron's Billy Brill, another Australian Lancaster pilot, Flight Lieutenant Dan Conway of No. 467 Squadron, also of Waddington, left the target on three motors.

About forty-five minutes after leaving Nuremberg on the way out of Germany, Conway's flight engineer, Sergeant Tanfield, reported that oil temperatures and pressures on the remaining port motor were 'off the clock'.

'He requested permission to feather the airscrew of the motor but as it still seemed to be running sweetly I decided that the gauges might be at fault,' Conway said. 'Particularly as flying on two motors all the way home didn't look like a proposition. I was right. We seemed to have plenty of petrol although here again the gauges were not registering.'

Flying Officer Dan Conway saw very little activity on the way home from Nuremberg apart from the usual search-lights. With the port outer stopped and the airscrew feathered, he had, like Brill, lost both airspeed and time. Lagging well behind the Main Force Bomber stream, and, anticipating a fighter attack at any time, he and his crew kept a good lookout.

Conway's flight plan called for him to cross the enemy coast on the way out over northern France and to make his English landfall near Beachy Head. When the navigator, Sergeant Joe Wesley, tried to get a positional fix by radar on his Gee-set he found that this also was unserviceable. All that Conway could do was maintain the DR course given him by Wesley, keep the Pole Star on his right and hope that they were on track with the rest of the bomber stream ahead of them.

After crossing the enemy coast without incident, Conway made his English landfall north of track, over the east coast of Suffolk where the special emergency landing ground at Woodbridge was 'a magnificent sight' with its flare path all lit up.

'It was now dawn,' said Conway. 'The navigator gave me a course for base. The airspeed indicator gave signs of reviving but could not be regarded as reliable. Fog was developing as we approached Waddington so I switched on our R/T and used the volume as a guide to the aerodrome. That, plus a lucky pinpoint, guided us home.'

Wheels and flaps down, Conway turned onto a final approach through the Lincolnshire fog with an exhausted crew bracing themselves. He had some trouble lining up on the runway and remembers that the approach must have looked 'spectacular'. Just before passing the control van by the runway he had to carry out a violent turn to stay aligned but landed smoothly and safely.

'At the debriefing we heard that approximately ninety-nine of our aircraft were missing,' he recalled. 'God knows how many more returned damaged. We were about the last in so we walked up to the mess with our WAAF Station Officer, a motherly and usually happy type who was most distressed at the losses. We had been lucky at Waddington though, as we only lost two or three aircraft.

'At breakfast one of the newer skippers—a fairly bumptious type at any time—was carrying on in a loud voice about the large number of scarecrow flares he had seen on the way in to the target. And this after hearing the losses. Ignorance is bliss.'

Understandably feeling 'fairly tired' after 8.30 hours of solid flying in solo command, and almost half of it on only three motors, Conway had a quick nap before setting out on a cross-country journey to visit old friends from flying training days at No. 27 OTU, Lichfield. Most of his crew he would meet later in London but Conway recalls that despite the Nuremberg losses—or perhaps because of them—it was 'quite a party' that night at Lichfield.

For Flight Lieutenant Stephen Burrows, of No. 44 Squadron, the journey home from Nuremberg was uneventful except for occasional searchlights and a little flak. About twenty miles from the coast on the way out, Burrows noticed, from his flight engineer's jump-seat alongside Wing Commander Thompson, a pair of light flak guns crossing their fire at about 10 000 feet. Even as he watched, a British aircraft caught 'a terrific packet' and crashed in flames.

Wing Commander Thompson, veteran of more than fifty operations over Germany, promptly dived his Lancaster for a low-level crossing of the enemy coast at about 100 feet and, when clear and out over the English Channel, climbed back up to 4000 feet. On the way across, the Lancaster had the company of a series of V1 flying bombs which passed by on the way to London.

'When we got nearer our coast we could see them exploding ahead', said Burrows. 'We did, incidentally, lose an engine while approximately a hundred miles inside enemy territory, due to some mechanical fault; this consequently made us late on arrival at base, which in turn prompted rumours that we were missing.

'Whilst I heard the rumour regarding leakage of information I must say, having had a little previous operational experience, it certainly appeared to me that Jerry was waiting for us. In fact it was said quite openly during the interrogation, with lots and lots of derogatory remarks being made. The debriefing was very quiet and the atmosphere electric.

'On return to base, and upon entering the Interrogation Room, our base commander, Air Commodore Pope ("Poppy"), a "dwarf" of a man of six feet six inches, and our station commander, Group Captain Butler, both asked me how the raid went and when I stated that I thought we had lost one hundred aeroplanes I was told not to be ridiculous and the doctor was told to ". . . send this crew on leave, it's time they had a rest!" However, as events proved, we lost ninety-four aircraft. Over breakfast there were quite a few empty seats with lots of spare fried eggs available. Very little sleep taken during the day and gallons of ale consumed in the evening.'

Summing-up on the Nuremberg operation, Burrows said: 'I would state that this raid was, without any doubt, the most severe experienced generally with seven aircraft missing from our unit, although we as a crew had had worse experiences on other trips.'

The way out of the target had been 'quite a sight' as Pilot Officer Ray Curling, RAAF, had seen it from the pilot's seat of his No. 622 Squadron Lancaster.

'We didn't need a navigator,' he reported. 'The moon lit the sky like daylight and vapour trails of aircraft ahead of us left a road like a modern highway. I just kept above this roadway in readiness to dive into its cover should the need arise. Fighter attack seemed to have eased off considerably. We were not permitted to land at our base, Mildenhall, and were diverted to the emergency airfield on the coast, Woodbridge. Landing there was no problem. There were plenty of other aircraft badly shot up. The various other air crews we spoke to confirmed our opinion that it had been a shocking raid.'

Curling's aircraft was undamaged. It had been airborne 8.00 hours.

(After the war an RAF medical officer expressed to Curling the opinion that the plan of the Nuremberg raid had been known to the Germans. 'Their attacks certainly seemed to confirm this,' commented Curling.)

After his Lancaster from No. 49 Squadron had successfully evaded flak, searchlights and fighters over Nuremberg, Flight Sergeant Walter Morrisby, RAF, reported that the first outward leg from the target was subject more to flak than to fighters. Although, from the flight engineer's jump-seat alongside Pilot Officer Clarke, he observed that German fighter flares by then were not as concentrated as before; he also observed fighter activity on the first long leg away from the target, south of Stuttgart.

The rest of the flight home was uneventful although the

French coast was not crossed as flight-planned, due to incorrectly forecast winds.

Morrisby and the crew who had been strangers to him, as he was flying a 'spare bod' trip with them, landed back at Fiskerton in Lincolnshire after 7.25 hours in the air.

Deep in southern Germany, somewhere near the cratered, smouldering wreckage of his crew's Lancaster, and far to the north of the outward-bound track of the mauled British bomber stream thundering home to England, Flight Sergeant Sidney Whitlock of No. 166 Squadron was facing up to the first few traumatic hours of a shot-down flyer's captivity. Initially came the stunned realization that his squadron mates would soon be safely and warmly abed at his base, Kirmington, long before he could possibly have stumbled even fifteen miles through the drifting snow and wind-whipped sleet of the hostile German night. After that came grudging recognition of the abysmal fact that, in only a few hectic seconds, his military status had suddenly degenerated from that of feared combatant to humiliated prisoner.

After being captured by armed civilians with leashed dogs, Whitlock was taken to a police station where he was joined by three other members of the crew as, one by one, they were rounded up—Flight Sergeant Watson, the bomb aimer, Pilot Officer Standen, the mid-upper gunner, and Sergeant Thrower, the rear gunner.

After hours of standing at the police station, with most of the local village population coming along to inspect them, Whitlock and his fellow crewmen were taken to a nearby country railway station. In a buffet there they encountered their Irish navigator, Flight Sergeant L. McCarney, and their pilot, Flight Lieutenant F. Taylor. McCarney had a broken leg and Taylor a broken thigh.

The two air gunners, Standen and Thrower, carried their pilot on a stretcher to a waiting goods train.

'Cradling arms with the bomb aimer, I carried the navigator who involuntarily screamed at every step, not having had his broken leg attended to,' Whitlock recalled.

By night-time on the day after Nuremberg, the airmen had arrived by freight train at a larger town where the pilot and the navigator were taken off to hospital and Whitlock, the two gunners and the bomb aimer were each put into separate cells.

At first light next day they were taken by train to a French POW camp where they were thoroughly searched to the extent of bending over with backsides bared. This was the first time they had been searched apart from an initial frisking of their flying gear.

Just forty-eight hours after being shot down they arrived at the Luftwaffe interrogation and transit camp Dulag Luft, at Oberursel near Frankfurt-on-Main, 'with civilians spitting on us,' as Whitlock recalled it. After that came documentation and solitary confinement in an overheated cell with barred, closed windows.

During interrogation it was made clear to Whitlock that many RAF crews had been shot down on the Nuremberg raid. It was also made clear by the interrogating officers that they knew far more about the operation than did Whitlock.

While at Dulag Luft he learned that his flight engineer, Sergeant J. Whitfield, and a new pilot, flying as co-pilot for operational experience before skippering his own crew, had both been killed.

Whitlock's pilot, Flight Lieutenant Taylor, had waited until the last possible moment for the slap on his thigh from the last member of the crew to leave the aircraft which was his own signal to bale out. Leaving it almost too late—too late, anyway, to get to the escape hatch in the nose—Taylor had gone out through the emergency escape-hatch in the cockpit, canopy above his head, and broken his thigh when his body hit part of the tail-plane structure of the aircraft. The navigator McCarney broke his leg when he dropped from a tree where he had been hung up by his parachute canopy.

Before Whitlock left Dulag Luft, interrogation officers told him that 132 British aircraft had been shot down on the Nuremberg attack. 'The transit camp was so full it could quite easily have been true,' he commented.

For Flight Sergeant Harry Webb in the mid-upper turret of his No. 640 Squadron Halifax, the trip home was uneventful, by contrast to the way into the target when his aircraft had been attacked five times by night-fighters. On the way out to the enemy coast Webb saw only a few lights and some occasional flak.

When the crew's flight engineer, Sergeant Mitchell, reported a fuel shortage, the pilot, Flight Sergeant Johnson, decided to land at Tangmere, instead of pressing on north to Leconfield in Yorkshire as it was suspected that a fuel tank had been holed during one of the night-fighter attacks. On landing, cannon-shell strikes were found in the wings, the fuselage and in both fins and rudders. The Halifax had been airborne for 7.45 hours.

After a brief sleep in strange surroundings instead of at their own familiar base, the crew flew thoughtfully home to Leconfield with the sun in their faces and the slipstream whistling through the jagged cannon-shell holes.

Ironically, after surviving Nuremberg with 94 aircraft lost, Berlin (72 lost) and Essen (58 lost), Harry Webb and his crew were destined to be the only RAF aircraft shot down just thirteen weeks later, during an attack on railway objectives at Dijons, a comparatively lightly defended, short-range target.

It was much quicker, of course, by Mosquito.

The way home from Nuremberg was enlivened for Flying Officer Harold Barker, DFC, RAAF, of No. 139 (Jamaica) Squadron, from the Pathfinder base at Upwood, by two warnings of enemy aircraft approaching from astern. Diving quickly, Barker's pilot, Flying Officer Allan Brown, RAF, soon lost them in his Mosquito Mark IV. They returned to Upwood without further incident having spent 4.35 hours in the air.

Reporting at de-briefing on combats which they had seen taking place in the bomber stream, Barker and his pilot agreed that the layer of cloud lit up by the fires in the target area below had made the heavy bombers an easy target for the swarms of fighters seen to be operating.

Sergeant Sidney Lipman, the eager flight engineer of No. 166 Squadron who was on his second operation after volunteering twice in the one evening to crew as a 'spare bod' replacement, flew home to Kirmington in Lincolnshire with some flak damage to his Lancaster. To his satisfaction he was able to log another 8.30 hours operational flying.

His crew in z-ZEBRA had been the last of the squadron's aircraft to land back at Kirmington and after de-briefing and breakfast he had returned to his hut to find his crew checking over his belongings. They had been told that z-ZEBRA was missing.

'I laughed,' said Lipman, 'and told them to put my gear back.'

No. 166 had lost four aircraft including one captained by Flight Lieutenant Proctor with whom Lipman had first volunteered to fly that night. The premature report that he had failed to return from Nuremberg proved to be a good omen for Lipman. Surviving that night he successfully completed a tour of operations with his own crew.

After nearly colliding head-on with an enemy fighter during the bombing run, the No. 625 Squadron Lancaster navigated by Pilot Officer Goldsmith, RCAF, had an uneventful trip home to Kelstern in No. 1 Group.

'I believe we used full power most of the way as we were shaken by seeing so many aircraft shot down,' Goldsmith said. 'After we landed we listened to the German news broadcast. They were claiming 135 of our aircraft destroyed. After what we'd seen we believed it.'

For Goldsmith and his crew their 13th trip had been a lucky one. Not so lucky were the crews of the four or five other Lancasters of the squadron which failed to return to Kelsgern that night from Nuremberg.

It was getting light when Flying Officer Sydney Johnson, RAAF, in his Lancaster x-XRAY returned to the Pathfinder base at Warboys, to be greeted by warnings that there were Bandits—intruding enemy aircraft—in the area. Not for this reason but because of 'duff weather', Johnson was diverted and landed at Marham, a Mosquito station, after 7.30 hours in the air.

In the 'Remarks' column of his pilot's log book Johnson

laconically recorded the salient details of the night's flight: 'Operations: Nuremberg. 780 aircraft. 96 lost. Primary blind marker. Duty carried out.'

Having flown out of the target area concealed in the contrail of another aircraft ahead of him, Pilot Officer Robert McHattie, of the special-duties Airborne Cigar unit, No. 101 Squadron, had hoped for an uneventful trip home, particularly with the track routed over occupied France once clear of Stuttgart and Karlsruhe. And so it was. Landing at Ludford Magna, McHattie and his crew were amongst several personally interviewed by the station commander after sectional de-briefing.

'He asked what sort of a trip we had had,' McHattie recalled. 'I told him that it had been pretty tough. Unfortunately I also told him about our difficulties with the mid-upper gunners' heating and the action I had taken in moving him out of the turret. I think my crew were shocked and I was hurt when he reprimanded me for having taken this action even if the gunner had remained operational at the heated astrodome position as a watchman.

'Emerging from the interview with the group captain, our spirits were further depressed to find that seven of our squadron's aircraft were missing, most of them from my own 'A' Flight. And so to breakfast and then to bed.

'Next day we found that as a result of our losses my crew had jumped from near bottom to the top of the 'A' Flight leave roster. Ah well, it's an ill wind . . .'

For Sergeant John Allison, wireless air gunner in Pilot Officer McHattie's Lancaster, the trip home from Nuremberg was remarkable mainly for the shock of learning, on return to his base, that the squadron had lost seven Lancasters.

'Amongst them was the crew that shared our hut,' he said.

At Ludford Magna, as at many stations of Bomber Command that night, Nuremberg had left its mark.

Curiously, Pilot Officer Arthur Bowman, of No. 463 (RAAF) Squadron, flying his Lancaster J-JIG, encountered very heavy flak near Strasbourg in France and again on the French coast as he headed home to Waddington in Lincolnshire.

He recalls that 'the de-briefing was very lively and all the crews had much to say about their experiences.'

After being attacked by fighters over the target, Pilot Officer Ronald Reinelt of No. 433 Squadron, Skipton-on-Swale, took his Halifax Q-QUEEN out on a homeward course down at about 11 000 feet and at reduced speed with a dead starboard outer motor, a windmilling prop and the prospect of fire reoccurring in the starboard wing fuel tanks.

During the agonizingly slow progress home, Reinelt's rear gunner Sergeant George Dykes kept anxious watch. Strangely, although it was almost daylight as the lame-duck Halifax limped home across northern France and although several airfields were passed where enemy aircraft were seen to be circling, the straggler was not intercepted and the French coast was reached without incident. Heading out over the English Channel, Dykes and his crew were delighted to have two RAF Spitfires join them, one either side, for the channel crossing.

Dykes' pilot, Ronald Reinelt, was awarded an immediate and well-earned DFC on safe return to Skipton-on-Swale.

After the free-for-all melee over the target, Flight Lieutenant Robin Knights, another pilot from No. 101, the special-duties squadron, was glad to get his Lancaster on a homeward heading. By then the unpredicted winds had scattered the bomber stream and with a long return flight over enemy territory it could be assumed that the German ground control interception controllers would be finding it easy to pick up stragglers. Certainly, Knights' gunners—Hart in the mid-upper turret and Murphy in the rear turret—kept him corkscrewing his Lancaster most of the way back to the coast so as to frustrate enemy fighters, whether real or imagined.

'Backplotting the navigator's log afterwards seemed to indicate that we had bombed Schweinfurt,' Knights said. 'I have my doubts as Germany is a big place on a dark night with no aids and the winds "up the spout". In retrospect, I wished that I had brought my bombs back.'

For the farm worker turned regular soldier turned officer

and pilot it had been an eight exhausting hours of night flying with three of them on instruments in turbulent cloud. It was all the more disappointing therefore not only not to have hit the primary target, Nuremberg, but also to finish the night with doubts about having hit Schweinfurt.

Having observed, on the way to the target, too many air-to-air combats and 'flamers' for his navigator to have had time enough to log, Pilot Officer Ern Mustard of No. 463 (RAAF) Squadron, Waddington, was not surprised to see signs of continued fighter activity along the straight homeward leg stretching from south of Stuttgart to north-east of Paris. There was certainly enough activity to keep him awake—and to keep the crew's minds off thoughts of going on leave. This, incidentally, was a factor which Mustard recalled as possibly being a contributory factor in the events of the night. Bomber Command had lately been calling frequently for maximum effort 'Goodwoods' with the result that many crews were long overdue for leave. At Waddington, during the Nuremberg briefing, all crews of Nos 463 and 467 squadrons had been promised leave on return to the base.

'If the situation was the same on other Bomber Command stations then there were a lot of tired men flying on the night of 30 March 1944,' said Mustard.

He recalled that at the de-briefing Squadron Leader Brill, 'B' Flight commander of No. 463 Squadron, already 'had the score' on the night's operations. When other pilots were estimating losses at thirty to fifty aircraft Brill was insistent they were nearer a hundred. It was Brill alone, also, who first reported sighting Ju 88 twin-engine night fighters with the *Schrage Musik* high-elevation cannons projecting from the top of the fuselage behind the cockpit for belly attacks. At Waddington this was thought to be the first occasion that the tactic had been used in a major way, not only on Ju 88 aircraft but also on the newer Me 410 twin-engine night fighters.

After 'a reasonable trip at above average height', Mustard went to bed. It was a shock to wake up about lunch-time next day and hear the final scores for Nuremberg,' he said.

Mustard and his crew had been spared to fly again for

many more nights, homing to Waddington before dawn with the familiar call-sign on the intercom as he called base for permission to land:

"Hello SLANGWORD, hello SLANGWORD, this is FULLER C-CHARLIE, FULLER C-CHARLIE."

Departing from the target a second time after its pilot had been lured back in by a false reading on a toppled gyro, Halifax EY-A of No. 78 Squadron, Breighton, settled down again at 0135 for the course to the French coast. Sergeant Davidson, the flight engineer, noticed that at last the contrails had stopped.

'It seems much darker now, away from the target,' his own narrative records. 'The wireless operator starts passing winds received from Group. They give 90 mph but the navigator does not agree. He makes the wind nearer 120 mph. Things are fairly quiet now and we seem all alone over Germany. Red TIs are seen on the ground as we pass well to the south of Aachen at 0300. On and on to the coast. Will we ever get there? There's a very bright star dead ahead. It could be Venus. 0430: the French coast is ahead, all black and gold. We are getting lower and lower but there is nothing to worry about. The navigator says our ground speed against the head winds is 64 mph. We could taxi faster. Coffee and biscuits never tasted so good before or since with the English Channel below. Beginning to relax now. It's been so quiet for the last hour.'

The crew's relaxation was premature for at this point the Halifax suddenly began to shudder and shake. Checking his panel, coffee forgotten, the flight engineer pin-pointed the trouble: the port inner engine was losing oil pressure and the engine rpm were surging. At 0450 he stopped the motor and feathered the airscrew. The Canadian skipper, Pilot Officer Christiansen, immediately asked the navigator for a course to the nearest airfield. Luckily, it turned out to be Ford, an emergency field on the south coast, positioned there for just such contingencies as this. Calling Ford as NOSMO A-ABLE, Christiansen was cleared to make a straight-in approach as by this time the Halifax had lost height down to about 500 feet above the sea. Joining the Ford circuit pattern at

0522, Christiansen wasted no time getting down and landed eight minutes later at 0530.

Ford was crowded with returning Lancasters and Halifaxes which had made emergency landings there. Davidson and his crew reported to flying control for de-briefing and Christiansen tried to telephone his base at Breighton, up north in Yorkshire, but the connection was poor so he made arrangements for news of his emergency landing to be passed on to No. 78 Squadron.

'All we want is food and sleep,' Davidson's account continues. 'Sleep, mostly. I feel as if I have been gutted. There's nothing inside me. Dirty and sweaty we go over to the mess. Lord, I think all Bomber Command is here. And the cigarette smoke! An LAC takes us to our billet, moaning all the way about making hundreds of beds and lighting fires. "What a bloody air force," he says. We don't care: "Where are the beds?" '

The crew finally tumbled into their beds at 0650. They had spent 7.20 hours in the air, 5.16 hours of it at 20 000 feet in temperatures of − 33 degrees Centigrade, and had breathed oxygen for 6.50 hours. They had taken off with 2046 gallons of fuel and landed with 86 gallons left, sufficient for little more than fifteen minutes flying.

The crew slept soundly. Seven hours later, on March 31, they were back at their aircraft where Davidson found a civilian ground engineer looking it over. When the civilian asked him where the crew had been the night before, Davidson said 'Nuremberg.'

'You lost ninety-six,' said the civilian who had been listening to the BBC.

Davidson stared at him, astounded. 'You must be kidding,' he said. 'It didn't look that bad to us.'

Inexplicably, the Halifax's port inner motor checked out satisfactorily on run-up. The previous night's malfunction was diagnosed as being due to coring up of the oil cooler on descent.

On return to Breighton, Davidson found that three of No. 78 Squadron's aircraft were missing—including Z-ZEBRA and H-HOW.

'Christ', thought Davidson, 'we went out to dispersal in

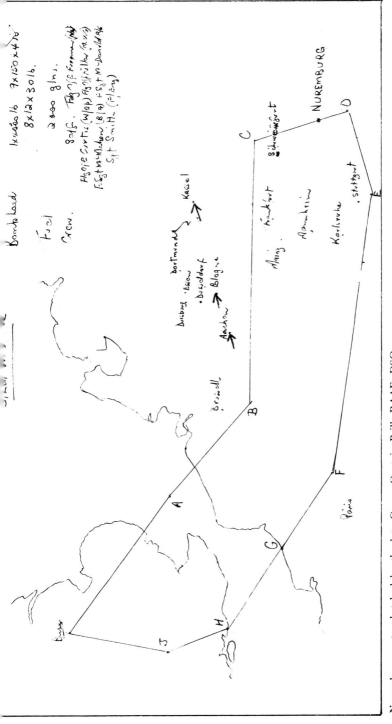

Nuremberg route, sketched by the late Group Captain Brill, RAAF, DSO, DFC and bar.

A Lancaster of No. 50 Squadron based at Skellingthorpe, Lincolnshire. *'Flight' magazine*

The late Group Captain W. H. Brill, RAAF, DSO, DFC and bar, who took part in the Nuremberg raid as a Lancaster pilot and flight commander of No. 463 (RAAF) Squadron, Waddington, Lincolnshire. When this war-time Air Ministry photograph was taken he had reached the rank of Wing Commander and was commanding his own squadron.   *Air Ministry*

the same crew bus as the crews of z-zebra and h-how.' He remembered talking with the rear gunner of z-zebra, flown by Sergeant Hampson. The crew had just returned from leave and this was their first operational flight.

There was little time for brooding, though, as the message from Ford abou a-able's emergency landing had not been received at Breighton and, on the assumption that Davidson's crew had also failed to return, all their personal gear had been put into store. They now sped to retrieve it.

Two years later Davidson was drinking a pint of beer in the sergeants mess at Catterick when he found himself talking to the rear gunner who had vanished from No. 78 Squadron with the rest of z-zebra's crew on their first trip, the one to Nuremberg. Over another pint of beer it transpired that the air gunner's Halifax had been attacked and set on fire just after crossing the French coast at 2334, only minutes ahead of Davidson's aircraft, and that Davidson had witnessed the action. Spirited return fire from the Halifax had scored strikes on the twin-engined German fighter which then broke off the attack and vanished. Getting no replies when he called on the intercom, the gunner climbed out of his turret and went forward to the nose of the Halifax. It was very draughty in the fuselage, with no member of the crew in sight. He found the cockpit empty and the forward escape hatch open. The crew had baled out. While there was still time to do so the gunner made his lonely way back to the rear turret and likewise parachuted out. Nuremberg, in terms of distance, and England, in terms of time, were suddenly a long way away.

For Davidson and his crew, an almost equally raw crew who had only ever flown over Germany once before, Nuremberg had truly proved to be their baptism of fire.

The long leg home from Nuremberg across a darkened Europe was remarkable to the Canadian navigator, Flying Officer Ronald Rudd of No. 429 Squadron, Leeming, for the mysterious appearance of a twin-engined Vickers Wellington, very close on the starboard side of Rudd's Halifax and in formation.

'Both gunners were a bit nervous,' Rudd said, 'but they didn't fire and he (the Wellington) veered off eventually.'

Wellingtons had long since been phased out as obsolete by Bomber Command except for their invaluable services in crew training at operational training units. Certainly no Wellington was included in the command's battle order for the night. Nor did the Luftwaffe admit to using any captured Wellingtons as observer aircraft during the Nuremberg operation.

Since the operationally experienced crew of the Halifax were hardly likely to mistake a Ju 88 for a Wellington, particularly at close range and in steady profile, it can only be assumed that the ghostly 'Wimpy' was from one of the RAF operational training units where selected crews who had done well during training were sometimes sent on leaflet-dropping 'Nickel' operations over occupied France as a preliminary to full-scale operations with a squadron.

For Flight Sergeant Reginald Parissien, of the Pathfinder unit based at Upwood, No. 156 Squadron, the air battle did not end as his Lancaster's bombs tumbled away over the target. As they turned for home, the wireless air gunner observed that the German attacks on the bomber stream were becoming even heavier.

'At times,' said Parissien, 'the air was full of flak, search-lights and silhouetted aircraft. Without doubt, and to the best of my knowledge, it was the moon that proved our greatest enemy. As we crossed the French coast and all at last was quiet, we realized that this had been a terrible night. We landed safely at our own station and at de-briefing gathered that although our own squadron's losses had been small, those of many others had been great. Many of our crews were telling of the aircraft they had seen shot down, some as many as twelve. At first we didn't believe them but, subsequently when more was revealed the day after we realized that they had been tragically right.'

Apart from sighting flak to starboard some twenty miles south of Stuttgart, Flying Officer William Barclay, also of No. 156 Squadron, had a quiet uneventful trip, including the way out to the coast which, as navigator, he logged having been crossed at 0357.2. Arriving over their squadron's base at Upwood at 0505 only to find it fogged in, the crew were diverted to Marham where they finally landed at 0533.

'. . . Nothing we saw on the trip suggested bad losses,' the Australian navigator noted, 'but this may have been due to our early timing. We found that flak and fighter activity livened up during the course of a raid and being in the fore-front we probably missed most of the fun, if that's what you could call it.'

Flight Sergeant Leonard Pratt of No. 427 (RCAF) Squadron, Leeming, flight engineer in Rex Clibbery's Halifax v-VICTOR, of 'B' Flight, recalled that there was no moon on the way out to the coast from Nuremberg.

Leaving the target Clibbery had turned sharply onto a leg to starboard. He then began to lose altitude rapidly so as to get the cover of the ground against possible fighter attacks as quickly as possible.

'I only remember one incident,' Pratt said. 'We were up at about two to five thousand feet and ahead we saw some tracer exchanged. A little while later we passed very close to an aircraft burning on the deck. One could see some sort of building, and trees, in the glow of the fire.'

Once out of the target area, and down at a lower level, Pratt manipulated his fuel system controls, draining the nearly empty tanks and reserving fuel in four main tanks, one for each engine, for landing. The enemy coast was re-crossed without trouble and the Halifax made its way north across England to Yorkshire only to be diverted, because of fog, to Stratford.

On their eventual return to Leeming—with Clibbery calling 'Hello ROSECREME, hello ROSECREME, this is HOLDTIGHT v-VICTOR, HOLDTIGHT v-VICTOR'—it seemed, by the empty dispersal pens and the familiar faces missing from de-briefing, that many other crews had also been diverted because of the fog which had cloaked Yorkshire.

It was then that the crew heard about Leeming's losses for the night which included both No. 427 Squadron's flight commanders, Squadron Leader Laird and Squadron Leader Bissett, who had captained two of the most experienced crews on the base. Laird was on almost the last trip of his first tour of operations and Bissett was already on his second tour. Harry Glass, a flight engineer with No. 429 (RCAF) Bison Squadron, which was also based at Leeming, was ultimately to be awarded the CGM for his behaviour after his aircraft had been shot up and had had to ditch.

So far as Pratt was concerned, Nuremberg was over. He went to sleep content in the knowledge that he had been able to achieve a 'pretty good' ratio of air miles per gallon.

Although Flight Lieutenant Reuben Wright, RCAF, had seen no German fighters on the way into the target, his rear gunner, Flying Officer Routledge, another Canadian, had at one time counted thirteen Lancasters or Halifaxes going down in flames south of Bonn on the way out. Back at No. 405 (RCAF) Squadron's base at Grandsden Lodge, the Pathfinder bomb aimer logged the fast time, for a Lancaster, of 6.50 hours. Nuremberg had been Wright's forty-eighth mission out of what was finally to be a total of sixty-two.

Sergeant Ted Shaw, RCAF, of No. 12 Squadron, came home to Wickenby in Lincolnshire with two blackened eyes and cannon shell fragments lodged in his left eye from the shell which had hit his rear turret on the run in to the target. He had also come home rather lower than usual for, having lost a lot of height while under attack and having bombed at a low level, Shaw's pilot had elected to come home at 3500 instead of 20 000 feet. On landing at West Malling, Kent, with the starboard inner motor stopped and the airscrew feathered, Shaw found that his gunnery partner in the mid-upper turret had hit the third attacker as he came in from dead astern and had blown it up. This rather compensated Shaw for having been on the receiving end of the enemy tracer. Both the pilot and the mid-upper gunner were awarded the DFM for their actions on this night during a flight which had lasted 7.15 hours.

In another temporarily three-engined Lancaster from Lincolnshire, Sergeant Joe Wesley of No. 467 (RAAF) Squadron, Waddington, found time dragging on the way out to the coast. Having bombed with the shot-up port outer

motor stopped and feathered, Wesley's pilot, Flying Officer
Dan Conway, had flown due south from Nuremberg for
about thirty miles, then turned onto a south-westerly course
and eventually almost due west.

'With only three engines we were losing height gradually
and felt very much a sitting duck,' Wesley said, 'but there
were no more personal incidents and the seemingly unending
journey home was uneventful.'

After having been airborne for 8.30 hours Joe Wesley's
Lancaster PO-K landed back at Waddington approximately
one hour overdue.

Flight Sergeant William Stenning, of No. 51 Squadron,
Snaith, reported that flak had been 'fairly bad' leaving the
target area and that the crew of Halifax MH-L had felt some
of the closer bursts. His pilot, Flight Lieutenant Joe Pawell,
the American in the RCAF, headed the Halifax around onto
the homeward course towards France and Belgium with the
aircraft just riding the cloud tops. They had barely settled
down on the new heading, with the target safely behind them,
when the rear gunner, Sergeant Jock Baxter, reported an
aircraft closing in astern, slightly below and partly in cloud.

'I got it on "Fishpond" and it was certainly moving in but
not fast,' said Stenning. 'I also reported to the pilot and he
started to corkscrew. As the contact was now visual and the
flight engineer could also see it, Jock was all set to fire from
the rear turret but something made him hold off. We lost
the aircraft in cloud and some argument arose as to whether
it was an Me 110 or a Lancaster as their twin tail fin arrangements were rather similar. We never did find out as the
aircraft finally disappeared for good.

'We must have been somewhere near Stuttgart when we
ran into searchlights and heavy flak. I poured out window
and we had a hectic ten minutes. This was about 0200. Soon
afterwards the flight engineer called me and asked me to help
him with the pilot who seemed half asleep and drugged. We
could not think he was wounded. Over the intercom he
mumbled "I'm OK. I'm OK. Get the wheels up." They
were down, we discovered—and so were we. Without realiz-
ing it we were down to only about 5000 feet instead of

20 000 feet. Something had gone wrong somewhere as fuel was very low on one tank and Alf Barnard, the flight engineer, had to do some quick calculating.

"We couldn't get the undercarriage up but the pilot seemed to be better and we were getting well over France. I got the trailing aerial out and tuned into 500 kc/s, just in case, and we headed for Tangmere, one of the emergency airfields in the south of England.'

Approaching the English coast Stenning could see a lot of activity with searchlights homing incoming bombers. By about 0345 the Halifax was over Tangmere where there appeared to be some confusion with Lancasters and Halifaxes milling about, flares going off and urgent Mayday calls crowding the air as bombers, diverted from their fog-bound bases further north, were stacked over Tangmere. In the middle of it all, Stenning's Halifax was diverted to Wing, near Silverstone. He promptly began working Wing HF/DF radio and got a bearing which he passed to Bob Clark, the navigator.

'About twenty minutes after leaving Tangmere,' said Stenning, 'the mid-upper gunner shouted that there were trees just below us and, sure enough, we were only a few hundred feet up. Great panic! The pilot was in a stupor again and would not respond quickly.

'We managed to get on a bit more boost and gained height again. All engines were OK but the wheels were still dragging. I later learned that the country we had flown over so low was Hindhead, only eight miles from my home, and its height above sea level had nearly finished us.

'By now it was half-light and very misty. At about 0400 we were approaching Wing airfield and got them on R/T. Visibility was bad but they were putting out goose-neck flares on the runway.

'We joined the circuit and made two attempts to get in. I went up by the pilot, with the flight engineer, but our help wasn't much good as each time he was sure he could do it but each time we overshot. Third time lucky and we were down—right on the goose-neck flares. I looked back from the astrodome and it looked like 'Fido' where we had knocked over some of the flares and the spilled paraffin had caught alight, burning all over the runway. The wheels had locked down OK.'

RAF Station, Wing, so named for its geographical location and not its place on any organization chart, then housed an operational training unit so it was with some pride—and not a little outright relief at being safely down on the ground again—that Flight Sergeant William Stenning underwent his first de-briefing as a member of an operational bomber crew just back from Germany. However, the crew's long trek from Nuremberg to their base at Snaith was not yet over.

Several other crews diverted to Wing reported worse trips than Stenning's crew had experienced but he and his crew were 'thunderstruck' when they heard on the BBC news at breakfast next morning that ninety-six aircraft were missing.

The pilot, Flight Lieutenant Joe Pawell, was still very ill and obviously not fit to fly but when the crew reported to flying control they were told they must leave for Snaith immediately. Pawell telephoned his base and was informed that the squadron had had no aircraft back at all from Nuremberg, via diversions, and that the crew might be required for operations again that night.

'As luck would have it,' Stenning said with some feeling, 'our own aircraft was unserviceable with a hydraulic line cut by flak and a fuel tank split open.'

Still tired, the crew collected rail warrants and set off for London but the train broke down and they did not get there until 4 pm. The RTO at the station contacted Snaith and got permission for the crew to stay overnight in London rather than travel on. The crew spent the night in luxury in the directors' quarters of Whitbread's Brewery where the navigator's father was chef. Next morning, with a parting gift of five hundred cigarettes from Colonel Whitbread, the crew set out again, this time from King's Cross where Stenning's wife had come to see him off after he had telephoned her.

There were three other Nuremberg crews in the north-bound train, all burdened with parachutes, Mae Wests, navigation and signals equipment and flying gear. The journey was uneventful until an inquisitive small boy accidentally pulled the ripcord of the parachute of the mid-upper gunner, Sergeant Wilf Matthews.

'Having bundled the canopy back into the bag and using his escape dagger to do it up, Wilf nearly cut his finger off,' Stenning said. 'The blood-stained parachute must have looked grim to the passers-by in the corridor.'

On arrival, finally, at Snaith the crew found that only six of the squadron's crews had survived the Nuremberg raid. The crew were sent on leave for four days but none too happily as it had been established that their pilot, Joe Pawell, had burst a duodenal ulcer while flying home from Nuremberg and had lost a lot of blood which, of course, explained his lapses into semi-consciousness at the controls.

'That finished his RAF career,' said Stenning. 'We were heart-broken. He was a most experienced pilot. Only twenty-nine, he had been flying since he was sixteen, in America, and had nearly 10 000 hours. He later returned to Philadelphia. We re-crewed with an Australian, Flying Officer Danny King, DFC, who had previously broken his back after colliding with the spire of Selby Cathedral, but for medical reasons he never completed his tour with us.'

Stenning and his crew were later informed that there had been a security leak on the Nuremberg operation and that German night fighters, rushed down from their bases on the Schleswig-Holstein peninsula, had been a major factor in the successful counter-attack by the Luftwaffe.

With his crew, Stenning went on to complete a tour of thirty-two operations with No. 51 Squadron.

Pilot Officer John Lambert, of No. 578 Squadron, Burn, in No. 4 Group, had landed without injury on the hard, frozen earth of a German field after he had been plucked from the escape hatch of Halifax LK-E when his parachute canopy had been prematurely snagged open inside the aircraft. Disposing of his parachute canopy and harness and flying gear, Lambert walked all that night through heavily wooded country and hid all the following day. The countryside was sparsely populated but, after a second night's marching, he was captured trying to steal food from a farmhouse near Hassfurt on the railway line between Bamberg and Stassfurt, about fifty miles north-west of Nuremberg.

After being taken to a Luftwaffe camp at Schweinfurt,

Lambert duly arrived at Dulag Luft, at Oberursel outside Frankfurt, where he saw the other two crew members who had parachuted with him—the bomb aimer, Pilot Officer Crate and the wireless air gunner, Sergeant Kay. Apart from the customary solitary confinement and interrogation, Lambert retained one dominating impression:

'The most demoralizing thing at Dulag Luft was that the interrogating officers seemed to have known every detail about the operation before it started and so the Luftwaffe had been able to inflict such severe punishment. They had detailed RAF maps on the walls with the exact flight plan shown. They also knew a great deal more about secret RAF navigational equipment than I did.'

Subsequently, at Stalag Luft VI in East Prussia, Lambert was to learn that his pilot, Pilot Officer Cyril Barton, RAFVR, had succeeded in navigating and flying the severely damaged Halifax back to England with the remaining crew members aboard—Flight Sergeant Trousdale, flight engineer; Sergeant Woods, mid-upper gunner; Sergeant Brice, rear gunner —but had been killed while attempting a forced landing at Ryhope, on the Durham coast south of Sunderland.

Pilot Officer Barton's return to England from Nuremberg is best described in the cool, unemotional prose of his citation to a posthumous award of the Victoria Cross.

'On the night of 30 March 1944, Pilot Officer Barton was captain and pilot of a Halifax aircraft detailed to attack Nuremberg. When some seventy miles short of the target the aircraft was attacked by a Junkers 88. The first burst of fire from the enemy aircraft made the inter-communication system useless. One engine was damaged when a Messerschmitt 210 joined the fight. The bombers' machine guns were out of action and the gunners were unable to return the fire.

'Fighters continued to attack the aircraft as it approached the target area and, in the confusion caused by the failure of the communications system at the height of the battle, a signal was misinterpreted and the navigator, air bomber and wireless operator left the aircraft by parachute.

'Pilot Officer Barton faced a situation of dire peril. His aircraft was damaged, his navigational team had gone and he could not communicate with the rest of the crew. If he continued his mission he would be at the mercy of hostile fighters when silhouetted against the fires in the target area and if he survived he would have to make a $4\frac{1}{2}$-hour journey home on three engines across heavily defended territory.

'Determined to press home his attack at all costs, he flew on and, reaching the target, released the bombs himself.

'As Pilot Officer Barton turned for home the propeller of the damaged engine, which was vibrating badly, flew off. It was also discovered that two of the petrol tanks had suffered damage and were leaking. Pilot Officer Barton held to his course and without navigational aids, and in spite of strong head winds, successfully avoided the most dangerous defence areas on his route. Eventually he crossed the English coast only ninety miles north of his base.

'By this time the petrol supply was nearly exhausted. Before a suitable landing place could be found, both port engines stopped. The aircraft was now too low to be abandoned successfully. Pilot Officer Barton therefore ordered the three remaining members of his crew to take up their crash positions. Then, with only one engine working, he made a gallant attempt to land clear of the houses over which he was flying. The aircraft finally crashed and Pilot Officer Barton lost his life but his three comrades survived.

'Pilot Officer Barton had previously taken part in four attacks on Berlin and fourteen other operational missions. On one of these, two members of his crew were wounded during a determined effort to locate the target despite appalling weather conditions. In gallantly completing his last mission in the face of almost impossible odds, this officer displayed unsurpassed courage and devotion to duty.'

Wing Commander D. T. Forsyth from Melbourne, Australia, the commanding officer of No. 466 (RAAF) Squadron, flying Halifax J-JIG, brought his crew safely back to Leconfield after a flight lasting 8.15 hours which had been 'absolutely free of trouble or incident.'

Forsyth's crew was another typical British Commonwealth cross-section: an English navigator, Warrant Officer Wooton; South African bomb aimer, Pilot Officer Jeffries; English flight engineer, Flight Lieutenant Nicholson; English wireless air gunner, Flight Sergeant Bennett; Australian mid-upper gunner, Pilot Officer Downton and English rear gunner, Sergeant Dent.

Wing Commander Forsyth said that his squadron lost no aircraft on the Nuremberg operation and he could recall no real damage to any aircraft. It was his recollection that this was the first Bomber Command operation of any size and depth of penetration carried out in the 'moon periods'.

He believed that the force's troubles began when quite a number of aircraft bombed the wrong target. After some time on the southerly leg of the course down to Nuremberg, he commented to his crew that he could see the target with an attack developing some 30° to starboard. The navigator, Warrant Officer Wooton, was quick to reply that this could not be Nuremberg. He was quite certain of his position, the aircraft was right on track and there were some minutes to go before reaching Nuremberg.

As Wing Commander Forsyth flew on south it was obvious that 'a not inconsiderable number' of aircraft were involved in attacking the wrong target.

'The effect was that the aircraft immediately turned onto a westerly heading for home.' he said. 'Thus the force was spread over a very wide area of Germany thus reducing considerably its strength and safety. The offending aircraft also doubtless flew over heavily defended areas instead of along the planned "safe" track home.'

Instead of celebrating his crew's successful return to RAF Station, Skipton Bridge, Yorkshire, from the long-awaited thirtieth and last trip of their tour of operations, Pilot Officer John McLauchlan, RCAF, of No. 433 Squadron, having narrowly escaped being impaled on the steeple of a medieval Nuremberg church as he parachuted into Germany, was to spend the rest of the night in a local Gestapo gaol.

Next morning he saw the wreckage of numerous British bombers still burning and smoking in and around Nuremberg so he was not unduly surprised when an interrogating officer at Dulag Luft subsequently told him that the Luftwaffe had shot down 178 British aircraft during the battle of Nuremberg. He was even less surprised to be told that the Germans had known in advance not only the target but also the track of the bomber stream. Of the nearly seven hundred British aircrew shot down, McLauchlan encountered less than twenty fellow survivors during his stay in the transit camp at Dulag Luft. This could have been due to the fact that British survivors of combats during the running air battle had been scattered along the bomber stream's route for at least five hundred miles.

Security was also being questioned back in England by crews now safely returned from Nuremberg but still visibly shaken by the ferocity and accuracy of the Luftwaffe's counter-attack. The subject was raised during de-briefing of crews at Binbrook, in No. 1 Group, where Pilot Officer Samuel Moorhouse of No. 460 (RAAF) Squadron had landed at 0527 with only seven more trips to fly before completing his tour of operations. As navigator in Pilot Officer Howell's Lancaster L-LOVE he had been too busy calculating, plotting and estimating actual wind velocities for broadcast back to base to have time to observe much of the action occurring outside the aircraft until the French coast was re-crossed between Calais and Le Havre.

After 7.30 hours of navigating under imminent threat of interception and attack, particularly as the moon climbed higher, Moorhouse was tired on return to Binbrook. Not so tired, though, that he did not have a brief but specific memory of the reaction of many of the Binbrook crews:

'My recollection of the de-briefing is confined to the general opinion expressed by the crews that there had been a leakage of information so far as the route was concerned, particularly between Cologne and Frankfurt.'

Another Lancaster navigator, Flying Officer Harry Mackinnon, of East Kirkby's No. 57 Squadron, in Lincoln-shire, recalled that the Nuremberg night was memorable as being the only operation he ever flew when time went so slowly. Normally he was working desperately hard against time but on the long, homeward course from 48° 30′ North, 09° 20′ East—south of Stuttgart, to 49° 20′ North, 03° 00′ East—near Paris, he estimated the Lancaster's ground speed against bucking head-winds as only 120 knots and it seemed as if the leg would never end.

'On this leg,' he said, 'the crew, as usual, asked when we would get to the coast. Naturally I was in the middle of a calculation and irritably answered, "Oh, about an hour". Some hundred miles further on, they asked again. This time I had the exact answer—just over $1\frac{1}{2}$ hours. I could feel the chilling reaction of the rest of the crew. They never really forgave me.'

Mackinnon and his crew went on leave next day and on his way home in the train to Birmingham, Mackinnon was asked by an elderly lady whether Bomber Command had been out on operations the previous night and whether any aircraft were missing. He was always to remember the expression on her face when he said, 'Oh, about ninety-six'. He then fell asleep.

Only one Lancaster from No. 57 Squadron, flown by Flight Lieutenant Tickler, failed to return. It had been the crew's eleventh sortie.

It was Mackinnon's recollection that Bomber Command called in all navigator's logs after the Nuremberg operation for analysis and evaluation by the Command's operational research section. Mackinnon's own opinion was that the heavy losses were due to having had 'a bit of a moon'.

'You could see for miles,' he said, 'and then there was the long time spent over enemy territory on the way back due to the head-winds. This was, of course, Bomber Command's heaviest loss. Second was a raid on Munich earlier in 1944 with, I think, 79 lost, and third was Berlin on 24 March, six nights before Nuremberg, with 76 missing.'

After having taken his not very experienced crew into and out of the Nuremberg target area on his sixty-sixth heavy bomber mission, Wing Commander Pat Daniels, commanding officer of No. 35 Squadron, found that the German fighters were not as much in evidence on the way out to the French coast.

After 7.20 hours airborne in his Lancaster s-SUGAR, Daniels landed at his Pathfinder base at Gravely to be greeted by Air Vice-Marshal D. C. T. Bennett, founder and ranking leader of the Pathfinder Force, who had come to Gravely to attend de-briefing of the crews.

'I told him this would be the biggest chop ever,' Daniels said.

Bennett replied, 'Pat, you always exaggerate everything.'

As Daniels dryly put it: 'I believe I was later proved to be correct.'

Although Sergeant Howard Beddis, of No. 103 Squadron, Elsham Wolds, did not see a single enemy fighter during the 8.30 hours that his Lancaster was airborne on the Nuremberg raid, ironically he was to be shot down eleven nights later on 10 April during a pre-invasion railway attack on the far less formidably defended target of Amiens in France.

None of the Luftwaffe officers who interrogated the RAF flight engineer even mentioned the Nuremberg air battle. Already, in the fire and fury of the massive European air war, Nuremberg was by then only history.

Pilot Officer Donald Richardson, of No. 50 Squadron and navigator of Lancaster VN-F, returned safely to his base at Skellingthorpe, Lincolnshire, where his rear gunner, Sergeant Bacon, reported having seen many combats south of the Ruhr on the long leg out of France and across the Rhine into Germany.

'We ourselves were never touched,' said Richardson.

Pilot Officer Philip Plowright, of No. 9 Squadron and pilot of another No. 5 Group Lancaster from Lincolnshire, returned to his base at Bardney where he concluded his log-book entry for the eight-hour flight with the single comment: "Ninety-nine aircraft lost".

Buffeted by blast from flak bursts over the target, Sergeant Eric Morrey's Lancaster JO-B, from No. 463 (RAAF) Squadron, survived the barrage without being hit. Soon the Lancaster was flying in smooth air with speed building up as the captain, Pilot Officer Charlie Cassell, RAAF, gradually lost height on the way out to the French coast.

Once over the English coast the flashing identification

beacons of friendly airfields, dotted about in the darkness below, were a comforting greeting. Soon the Waddington flare path was in sight, south of the dark, many-spired bulk of Lincoln Cathedral, that familiar landmark to all who flew from the fen country in No. 5 Group.

'Charlie was soon making his final approach using all four throttles to regulate the rate of descent,' said Plowright. 'As flight engineer I made a final check to see that the wheels were securely locked in the down position. We were now 600 feet over the outer marker beacon and Charlie asked for full flap. A screech of tyres and we were rolling up the runway. After such a long night—it was now 0620 after having been airborne for eight hours since 2220 the previous night—Charlie had made an exceptionally good landing.'

With the Lancaster parked, bomb-doors open ready for re-loading and all four faithful Merlins switched off, Plowright and his crew were quickly and thankfully out of the aircraft and on their way to de-briefing. The flight engineer noted that after the mixed tension and boredom of the long flight the crew seemed to be in unusually high spirits.

Sergeant James McLean, of No. 9 Squadron and mid-upper gunner in Flight Lieutenant Pearce's Lancaster F-FOX, was conscious not of flak but of increased fighter activity after leaving the target.

'We observed a number of aircraft shot down,' he said, 'but as we were still flying slightly off track we had no trouble at all on the way out to the coast. I remember that, as a crew, we estimated having seen a total of about forty aircraft shot down in flames and these mainly on leaving the target. Our flight home to Bardney was uneventful apart from some flak and we landed back at base undamaged having been in the air for eight hours and twenty minutes.'

Among the British aircraft attacked by fighters on leaving the target was Sergeant Geoffrey Jennings' Lancaster G-GEORGE from No. 630 Squadron, East Kirkby. From his station in the mid-upper turret, Jennings was able to witness the development of simultaneous attack by two fighters:

'The rear gunner reported one approaching from astern and I observed what I believed to be an Me 110 coming in directly on the starboard side. I gave the order to dive to starboard and as we dived I endeavoured to open fire but my guns were frozen up. However, the prompt evasive action of our skipper, Peter Nash, was sufficient to get us out of trouble and we were not engaged again. It was obvious by the amount of tracer flying around that many engagements were taking place. We observed one or two of our aircraft going down out of control after leaving the target area.'

The way out to the coast from Nuremberg was no armchair ride for one Lancaster crew from No. 622 Squadron, Mildenhall, in No. 6 Group, whose narrative was made available by Mr M. A. Garbett. From it emerges a brief but realistic picture of what a bad trip in a bomber could be like.

'At 0217 rear gunner reports fighter to port quarter at 1000 yards but it makes off. At 0221 our aircraft is violently attacked, without warning, and cannon shells smash through the port side of the fuselage penetrating the navigator's neck and chest killing him instantly. The navigational instruments are wrecked. The flight engineer's panel is unserviceable. The bomb aimer and myself struggle aft to the rest-bed with the navigator's body. The bomb aimer then binds the wounds to stop blood dripping on the floor of the aircraft.' [Fluids such as blood, vomit, coffee spilled from in-flight ration flasks or oil gushing from the ruptured pipelines of a shot-up hydraulic system could make the metal deck above the Lancaster's bomb bay slippery and dangerous to walk on, particularly when the aircraft was engaged in evasive manoeuvres.]

'When we were hit, the aircraft lost 7000 feet, out of control, but the skipper kept his head and with difficulty regained control and set course on DR. The bomb aimer makes a reasonable effort at navigating. The port outer motor is practically shot out. Number three fuel tank is holed. A test on the undercarriage fails to extend the legs. Flaps also fail to extend.

'The English coast is a welcome sight. Called up Woodbridge for priority landing and warned them to stand by for crash landing . . . whole crew bruised on aircraft's violent impact with ground.

'The aircraft is a total wreck and we have difficulty getting the dead navigator out owing to a floor spar which is pinning him down. We thank the skipper and shake his hand. The mid-upper gunner had disappeared. The bomb aimer found him out on the concrete dispersal. He was dead.'

For Flight Sergeant Roger Callaway, the Canadian rear gunner of Halifax OW-N of No. 426 Squadron, withdrawal from the contested target area was a quiet affair subsequently complicated only by the urgent need for the pilot, Flight Lieutenant Shedd, to visit the Elsan—literally the can—at the rear of the aircraft. During this embarrassing manoeuvre with the controls of the Halifax in the hands of the flight engineer, the aircraft got slightly off course over France and flak opened up as OW-N flew over a Luftwaffe airfield. The field's runway lights were then switched on and Callaway and his crew surmised that more night fighters were taking off. After this incident the crew saw several more aircraft shot down.

'Other than for this,' said Callaway, 'it had only seemed like just another long trip but we were naturally saddened by the number of missing faces at beer call. Our squadron used to buy beer for our missing friends then lean their chairs back against the table and God help anyone who tried to sit in the places of those missing.'

It was Callaway's recollection that among those missing from the messes of the airfield at Linton-on-Ouse that night were all of No. 426 Squadron's section leaders—bombing, navigation, signals, engineering and gunnery—who had been flying as a single crew.

After a trip which had gone smoothly because he had been consistently close on the heels of the Pathfinders and ahead of the bomber stream, Pilot Officer Frank Collis of No. 207 Squadron flew his Lancaster V-VICTOR south for eight minutes after leaving the target. Then he turned west to track between Stuttgart, Karlsruhe and Strasbourg. By 0400 he had re-crossed the French coast near Dieppe at 15 000 feet on a course of 310° Magnetic and continued descending to 10 000 feet over the English Channel. Navigation lights were switched on again as he crossed the English coast to the west of Beachy Head. After that it was Reading and Peterborough, then finally, at 0517, the beckoning flare path of Spilsby base, inland from Skegness.

Collis landed at 0525 after 7.25 hours airborne on what he described as 'a somewhat easier trip than usual' with no damage at all to his aircraft.

'We were all surprised,' he said, 'to learn on the following day that ninety-four aircraft had been shot down or, more accurately, were missing. It seems possible that there might have been a leak in security.'

Although Collis could not recall whether No. 207 Squadron lost any aircraft he added cautiously, 'We did not operate very often without losses'.

He was not exaggerating. On this occasion two Lancasters of No. 207 Squadron failed to return to Spilsby: ND 586, flown by Pilot Officer J. H. Thornton, RCAF; and LM 436, flown by Pilot Officer B. C. Riddle, RNZAF.

It was fog over England, not flak or fighters over Europe, that was nearly the undoing of Lancaster U-UNCLE of No. 622 Squadron, on its return from Nuremberg. Navigated by Flight Sergeant Edgar Hazelwood, the Lancaster arrived back over its base at Mildenhall in Suffolk only to find the airfield blanketed by ground fog. The pilot, Flight Sergeant McQueen, was then instructed to divert to Docking, north of King's Lynn, on The Wash.

'We landed with enough fuel in our tanks for a further five minutes flying,' Hazelwood noted. 'I understand a number of our aircraft crashed over England due to lack of fuel and being unable to land at their bases because of fog.'

After experiencing and witnessing German fighter attacks from the coast to Nuremberg, J. H. Maxwell, the RCAF navigator with No. 97 (Pathfinder) Squadron, Bourn, reported no fighter engagements over the target where the Lancaster's Parramatta ground marker flares were dropped. Continuing ten miles to port of track on the way home, he observed many more combats on the track out to the coast. Maxwell logged 7.10 hours for the flight.

'I believe our squadron put out about twelve aircraft of which our losses were seven,' said Maxwell. 'I remember this particular raid because, upon return, the losses were so heavy we were taken off operations until 11 April 1944 to allow crews to be posted from the OTU and Lancaster aircraft to be delivered to the squadron from the manufacturer.'

Having dived to blow out the fire in the bomb-bay after a night fighter's attack from below, and then flown on to Nuremberg without his jettisoned bomb-load, Pilot Officer Henry Forrest of No. 9 Squadron returned home to Bardney with a dead mid-upper gunner but 'without further incident'.

It would have been with infinite relief that his crew finally heard him calling base for landing instructions: 'Hello SMALLTYPE, hello SMALLTYPE. This is ROSEN VICTOR, ROSEN VICTOR.'

With characteristic brevity, Squadron Leader Arthur Doubleday of No. 467 (RAAF) Squadron, recorded his own return to Waddington: 'I can distinctly recall a sharp deterioration in the weather after return to base but this did not affect me personally.'

It was Squadron Leader Doubleday's belief that the 'relatively heavy losses' suffered on the Nuremberg operation were due to three factors: the presence of almost continuous condensation trails; a three-quarter moon; and the fact that the target was flight-planned across one of the best, if not the best, fighter control sectors in Germany.

Nuremberg or not, though, the Australian flying partnership of Brill and Doubleday was still very much in business.

Now it was the last day of March. With the dawn, the massacre was over.

Bomber Command had been hurt—grievously hurt—but the great force would lick its wounds as it had done before, shake its head and sharpen its claws to fight another night over Germany and all the nights after that until, at last, came the first amazed dawn of peace.

6 The Reckoning

The Allied effort

A total of more than 5250 Bomber Command aircrew took off to attack Nuremberg.

● The Main Force component of the bomber stream consisted of 676 aircraft—462 Lancasters and 214 Halifaxes. The Pathfinder Force employed 110 Lancasters and 9 Mosquitoes.

● The entire Bomber Command force, both Main Force and Pathfinders, totalled 795 aircraft, of which 616 attacked the primary target at Nuremberg.

● Of the 119 Pathfinder aircraft which took off, 96 attacked the primary target, 6 returned early and 11 failed to return.

● Of the 94 British aircraft which failed to return to their bases, 62 were shot down by enemy fighters, 14 were brought down by flak, 2 were lost in collisions and 16 were listed as missing because of unknown causes.

● Of the total aircraft lost 64 were Lancasters and 30 were Halifaxes.

● Losses sustained by the bomber groups were: No. 1 Group, 21; No. 3 Group, 8; No. 4 Group, 20; No. 5 Group, 21; No. 6 Group, 13; No. 8 Group (PFF), 11.

The following squadrons of Bomber Command took part in the operation:

No. 1 Group: Nos. 12, 100, 101, 103, 166, 460, 550, 576, 625 and 626.

No. 3 Group: Nos. 15, 75, 80, 115, 149, 199, 514 and 622.

No. 4 Group: Nos. 10, 51, 76, 78, 158, 466, 578 and 640.

No. 5 Group: Nos. 9, 44, 49, 50, 57, 61, 207, 463, 467, 617 and 630.

No. 6 Group: Nos. 408, 420, 424, 425, 426, 427, 429, 432 and 433.

No. 8 Group: Nos. 7, 35, 83, 97, 105, 109, 139, 156, 405, 582, 627 and 692.

The weather conditions actually encountered by the crews are described below:

At the bases the weather was fit until 0400 hours when snow and sleet became widespread; then 7/10 convection cloud was experienced on the English coast, 4/10 strato-cumulus over Belgium and thence little cloud to twenty miles north of the target where 7/10 to 10/10 thin medium cloud was met. On the return flight there was 6/10 cloud up to 10 000–15 000 feet, gradually lowering to 4000–18 000 feet over north-east France. Over Nuremberg 7/10 thin medium cloud in thin layers to 15 000–17 000 feet was met with patchy cirrus at 22 000 feet. Through breaks in the cloud visibility was good. The wind speed was 35 mph in direction 280° at a height of 21 000 feet increasing to 60 mph towards the target and 70 mph over the French coast on the way home. The surface wind at the target was light and variable.

Although the RAF was unable to establish how many Bomber Command aircraft ditched in the sea on the return flight, seven were known to have been wrecked beyond repair in landing or taxiing accidents as weather deteriorated at the bases.

A total of 2460 tons of bombs was dropped, consisting of 1069 tons of high explosive and 1391 tons of incendiaries.

The 676 Lancasters and Halifaxes of Main Force were laden with a total of approximately 1 352 000 gallons of fuel.

For the guns of their front, mid-upper and rear turrets they carried 5 408 000 rounds of belted .303 ammunition, a thousand rounds per gun, with a total weight of about 225 tons.

Gunners of the Lancasters and Halifaxes claimed a total of 7 German night fighters certainly destroyed before

Nuremberg was reached and also claimed 2 probably destroyed and 9 damaged.

Because of insufficient photographic evidence it was not possible to evaluate the results of the attack on Nuremberg but, on analysis of such evidence as was available and from statements by crews at de-briefings, it became clear that the bombing had spread widely downwind to the east of the target. A German report issued after the raid indicated that damage was caused and population losses suffered in the built-up area of Nuremberg and several other localities.

Generally, a report stated after the war, Bomber Command experienced little trouble from ground defences during the course of the operation. Over the target, the searchlights of Nuremberg could not penetrate the cloud and heavy flak was fired in moderate barrages at 19 000–22 000 feet. Light flak fired to 15 000 feet was rather more intense.

As for the then-known battle order of the Luftwaffe nightfighter force on the night of 30 March 1944, an estimation of the scale of the effort put up by the Germans indicated that four night-fighter wings—NJGs 1,3,4 and 6—with elements of two other fighter formations were engaged in the Nuremberg action. Details of claims and losses subsequently extracted by British researchers from the German Air Situation Map of 30 March 1944, are as follows.

The Luftwaffe effort

● I Korps put up 54 single-engined Wilde Sau fighters, 5 Himmelbett fighters, 100 controlled Zahme Sau fighters, 64 non-controlled Zahme Sau fighters and 23 illuminator aircraft including 4 as observers, a korps total of 246.

● 7 Division operated 3 Himmelbett fighters, 5 controlled Zahme Sau fighters, 5 Wilde Sau fighters and 2 illuminator-observer aircraft—a divisional total of 15.

● II Korps committed 16 Himmelbett fighters and 25 controlled Zahme Sau fighters, a korps total of 41.

● Of the grand total of 302 Luftwaffe aircraft airborne, 59 were Wilde Sau; 24, Himmelbett; 130, controlled Zahme Sau; 64, non-controlled Zahme Sau; and 25, illuminators and observers.

The Luftwaffe claims

● In I Korps, the Wilde Sau single-engined fighters claimed 4 certain and 3 probable victories; the Himmelbett aircraft claimed one certain. The controlled Zahme Sau fighters claimed 48 certains and 3 probables; the non-controlled Zahme Sau crews also claimed 48 certains.

● In 7 Division, controlled Zahme Sau fighters claimed 2 certains and 1 probable.

● In II Korps, Himmelbett fighters claimed 3 certains and controlled Zahme Sau fighters claimed 11 certains and 1 probable.

● Of the total of 134 Lancasters and Halifaxes claimed as certainly destroyed 17 were attributed to the flak defences with 16 certains by Flak Luftflotte Reich and 1 by Flak Luftflotte 3.

The disparity between the British admissions and the German claims on Bomber Command's losses were subsequently the subject of rather acid comment in the May 1963 issue of *Jagerblatt* (*Fighter Talk*), the official journal, published in Frankfurt-on-Main, of the Society of Fighter Pilots whose membership includes many former Luftwaffe night-fighter pilots and crewmen.

The German writer stated: 'One of the most disastrous night missions of the RAF was the attack on Nuremberg on the night 30 March 1944. The OKW Report of the next day claimed the destruction of 134 British planes during the night. Official English statements were reporting 96 planes as lost or missing and 17 which had crashed near their bases and were consequently beyond repair. The apparent difference between the German and English figures is best commented upon with this British statement:

"I know that a number crashed into the sea or near their bases. These, however, are not in the official count of missing planes because it is known where they are and are, therefore, not missing"!'

Such a statement, certainly, is somewhat reminiscent of *Catch 22*.

The Luftwaffe losses

A curious feature of the German casualty list was the high proportion of missing aircraft—11 from I Korps and 1 from II Korps. Only 4 destroyed aircraft were found—2 each from I Korps and 7 Divisions. Five landed damaged—4 in I Korps and 1 in 7 Division. No personnel were listed as killed or wounded. Presumably the missing crews went down over the remoter and more sparsely settled areas of the most mountainous regions of southern Germany. Fuel shortage was a constant hazard for the single-engined Wilde Sau fighters—Fw 190 and Me 109 aircraft—when operating at night. Significantly, all but one of the 12 aircraft reported missing came from I Korps which had been operating nearly all the 59 Wilde Sau fighters flung into the battle that night. The fact remains, though, that for a total of 12 fighters reported missing and 5 destroyed, the Luftwaffe night-fighter force had acquitted itself with great skill, determination and success.

Though no less determined, a high percentage of the equally skilled British crews had not been as successful in the achievement of their stated objectives for the night, if a contemporary air raid report by police headquarters in Nuremberg is to be regarded as accurate. It at least confirms that the mad March winds had been responsible for much of the disarray of the bomber stream on its approach to the target.

The document reported on the night's events in Nuremberg from 0035 to 0222.

It stated that the RAF attack lasted for thirty minutes from 0102 to 0132 and was carried out by 200 aircraft in three waves with bombing directed against the eastern or downwind sector of the city.

The number and types of bombs dropped on Nuremberg were estimated as 300 large high-explosive bombs, 550 medium high-explosive bombs, 18 mines, 28 000 1.7-kg stick incendiaries, and 5000 phosphorus incendiaries.*

Pyrotechnics dropped by the Pathfinder Force included 60 red target-marker bombs and 50 flares.

---

*The only phosphorus in these bombs was in the small igniters. (See David Irving, *The Destruction of Dresden*, William Kimber, 1963.)

Eleven of the British high-explosive bombs failed to detonate.

Casualties were 74 killed and 122 wounded.

Of 54 people buried alive at seven different places in the city, 47 were recovered alive and 7 were dead on recovery.

Rendered homeless were 2400 people, 700 of them for a long period.

Totally destroyed were 130 buildings, 243 were heavily damaged, 879 moderately damaged and 2505 slightly damaged.

Both the British and the German accounts confirm that Bomber Command had indeed taken a battering.

However, in terms of percentages of battle casualties, Bomber Command had suffered and survived far worse losses including even the Command's historic first attack of the war on 4 September 1939, against German naval units off Brunsbuttel, in the Schillig Roads, and entering Wilhelmshaven. Out of a total of 24 Wellingtons and Blenheims, 7 failed to return—a far higher percentage loss rate than on Nuremberg.

Successively, in Fairey Battles, Bristol Blenheims, Lockheed Venturas, Douglas Bostons, de Havilland Mosquitoes, Armstrong Whitworth Whitleys, Handley Page Hampdens, Vickers Wellingtons, Avro Manchesters, Short Stirlings, Handley Page Halifaxes and Avro Lancasters, the tactical and strategic bomber crews of the RAF had known greater percentage losses than on the night of 30 March 1944, and would know them again.

For example, fourteen weeks after his participation in the Nuremberg operation, Pilot Officer E. A. Mustard of No. 463 (RAAF) Squadron was to take part in an attack on the small French town of Revigny-sur-Ornain, barely a hundred miles east of Paris. On the same day approximately 7000 tons of bombs were dropped by nearly 2000 British and American aircraft on Colombelles, a suburb of Caen on the invasion front, and by comparison the raid on railway targets at Revigny by 80 Lancasters from No. 53 Base, Waddington, was a small affair. There were four other attacks of similar scale that night on oil targets in the Ruhr and railway targets in France and Belgium. Since the Germans could not cope with them all they concentrated their attention on the Revigny operation: of the 80 British bombers from Wadding-ton, 27 failed to return.

'It was my thirty-fourth trip and it frightened me,' was Mustard's frank comment.

Mainly, it was the sheer outright weight of losses of aircraft and crews which was to make Nuremberg a night to remember if only for the surviving crews of Bomber Command: how were they to know that it would not happen again on the same disastrous scale the next night they took off for Germany. For those crews who had had a quiet trip to Nuremberg it was also memorable for the boredom and the weariness of the deep-penetration flight.

That such mass destruction of men and machines did not happen again was due, perhaps, to the intervention of a variety of factors and events beyond the control of either the RAF or the Luftwaffe.

The fact remains that many of the British crews' reactions to the Nuremberg 'massacre' were subsequently typified by the comment by Pilot Officer Dan Conway, of No. 467 (RAAF) Squadron:

'During those winter months of early 1944 I had the feeling that the Germans had only to come up with a new tactic, secret weapon or what-have-you, to knock off in one night a third or a half of our force. They had a good try at Nuremberg and for that matter we had lost about seventy on Berlin a week before. No wonder we went on, in April, to second-front targets in France.'

Regardless of the reckoning one thing was clear—for Bomber Command, RAF, the wild and windy month of March 1944 may have come in like the traditional lion, but it had certainly not gone out like a lamb.

7   The Headlines

Despite the limitations necessarily imposed upon British editors by the restrictions of war-time censorship and security regulations, the press reaction to the RAF losses on Nuremberg was neither inhibited nor soothing.

Notably realistic in its appraisal was the weekly British aviation journal *The Aeroplane*. This was not surprising. Along with its equally authoritative contemporary, *Flight*, the Jane cartoon strip (often literally so) in the London *Daily Mirror*, the deservedly popular pocket magazine *Lilliput* and the uproarious yet instructive misadventures of Pilot Officer Prune and his witless crew in the Air Ministry's training publication *Tee Emm*, *The Aeroplane* was widely read and respected by a vast majority of British, dominion, colonial and allied aircrew based in the United Kingdom during the war.

A regular feature was the weekly air war commentary, invariably hard-hitting and frequently written with almost Churchillian panache and waspishness in the trenchant traditions of the magazine's long-time editor and ardent advocate of air power, the late C. G. Grey.

The issue for 7 April 1944 was typical of the invariable war-time format. The feature, 'War in the Air', was dominated illustratively by a photograph of a US 8th AAF B17G landing after a daylight attack on Berlin—and by confirmation of the RAF's losses on Nuremberg:

'On Thursday night, 30 March, RAF Bomber Command sent a very strong force to Nuremberg and other targets in Germany. Conditions favoured the defence on this occasion. There was high cloud over most of the route but pilots flying within this encountered serious icing. On breaking out from cloud cover, the moon showed up the bombers' vapour trails and helped German fighters to pick them out. The enemy Air Command had made no mistake about Nuremberg being our target for the night and RAF air crews met the strongest concentration of German night fighters yet recorded in any action over Germany. Ninety-four bombers failed to return but the force nevertheless achieved its task with complete success.'

Editorial comment on the Nuremberg operation did not gloss over the unpalatable facts. The conclusions which it drew brought nods of agreement in every bomber mess and every bomber crew-room in the United Kingdom where no airman in his right mind would have been rash enough to have made the smug assumption that the Luftwaffe was a spent force.

The commentary stated: 'British and American bomber crews have been somewhat bored of late by optimists who appeared to assume that the German fighter force in Europe was on its last legs. Nuremberg has demonstrated in no uncertain manner how formidable that force still remains. The Luftwaffe's general position is, without doubt, serious and must inevitably become more so in the very near future, but the wounded tiger is a dangerous animal.

'The loss of ninety-four bombers in a single night came as a shock to the British public, already getting a little blasé with regard to reports of allied air attacks on Germany. It is a stern reminder of the dangers constantly and cheerfully faced on our behalf by bomber crews of the Royal Air Force.

'Although the casualty rate at Nuremberg was higher than usual, the great force that went there achieved its task with complete success. A whole series of munition factories, quite irreplaceable for Germany at this stage of the war, was eliminated. A further step was made in the great work of cleansing the world from the German war disease for another septic patch has been cauterized by the RAF.

'In order to conserve fighters, the enemy has, on many occasions during the past few weeks, left defence to the ground guns but results have been disastrous for him. This saving-up of fighters has brought ruin upon aircraft-production centres for even strongest ground defence cannot deflect the powerful day and night blows of allied bombing.

'However much the Luftwaffe chiefs may wish to keep aircraft and experienced fighting pilots in reserve for the coming invasion it is obvious that the protection of German war industry must come first, now that so much of it has been destroyed. Thus, the position of the German Air Command at the moment is not an enviable one. Aircraft losses must be kept down because replacements are already becoming difficult and may eventually become impossible unless the closing down of German industry by allied air action can be stopped which appears unlikely . . .'

On the day following Nuremberg, according to a report subsequently published in the British *Weekly News*, Luftwaffe fighter pilot Oberleutnant Fritz Brandt was cruising along the Belgian coast when he noticed burning wreckage on the ground. Banking, he headed towards the heart of Germany. He needed no compass as he flew low across German-occupied Europe towards the 'Stuttgart gap' in Germany's air defence system: navigation was only too easy—a simple process of flying from one ground fire to another. Every few miles there was the wreckage of an aircraft, some still burning and sending out pinpricks of light as tracer bullets exploded in the heat. The 'navigation markers' that made a smouldering line across Europe to Nuremberg were the funeral pyres of the British aircraft that had failed to return.

The air correspondent of the London *Daily Sketch* commented: 'The Germans put up more fighters than ever before in their efforts to stop the RAF attack on Nuremberg on Thursday night but in spite of their efforts Nuremberg was saturated with a major bomb-load. Our loss of ninety-four bombers . . . was admitted in London last night to be heavy and no effort was made to minimize it. But it was pointed out that it must be considered as a bad night in the air offensive against Germany which is now being carried out on a gigantic scale and compelling the Germans to throw in everything they have got.

'So far the Germans have failed to inflict damage that has in any way halted the growth or reduced the striking power of the night offensive and it's unlikely that they will do so.

'Conditions favoured the defenders on Thursday night as four nights earlier they favoured the invading bombers which carried out an equally heavy assault on Essen for the loss of no more than nine aircraft. Icing conditions in dense cloud frequently forced our bombers attacking Nuremberg into clear moonlight above the cloud where they were good targets for the hundreds of German fighters.

'For practically the whole of the 1 100 miles round-trip, the bombers were battling against determined fighter hordes.'

Another journalist reported: 'An experienced pilot told me he had never seen so many fighters.'

Another pilot, Flight Lieutenant D. R. Donaldson*, of Brighton, Victoria, Australia, said the Germans dropped a new kind of flare. 'They were in threes and appeared to be in triangle,' he said. 'They burned for about five minutes and lit up the sky and cloud very brilliantly. In the middle of the attack on Nuremberg one large explosion which lasted some seconds was observed in the target area.'

The air correspondent of another London daily newspaper raised a topical issue: 'Why do RAF night bombers fly unescorted? This question is likely to arise following the loss of ninety-four bombers (not ninety-six as stated earlier) in Thursday night's Nuremberg raid.

'The answer is, simply, that night escorts are not practicable. Flying often through cloud in conditions of poor visibility, an escort of any strength would find the greatest difficulty in keeping contact with a scattered bomber force.'

Alternatively, he could have added, the night bombers and any escorting fighters would have had the greatest difficulty in not making contact in the form of mid-air collisions which had always been an operational hazard from base to target and back again.

Whether it was due to a rare mood of benevolence prevailing at Bomber Command headquarters or whether it was due to the dictates of pre-invasion bombing strategy is not known but the next time Bomber Command took off,

*Flight Lieutenant Donaldson's navigator was Flight Sergeant J. G. Earl, of No. 460 (RAAF) Squadron, whose own recollections are included elsewhere in this narrative. Subsequently, as a wing commander, Donaldson commanded the Australian Governor-General's Flight, based at RAAF Station, Canberra, ACT, Australia.

six nights later on 5 April, it was not for Germany but for France where aircraft factories and repair depots near Toulouse were attacked. No opposition was encountered over France and the force returned without loss.

Bomber Command went again to France on the night of 9 April to attack railway targets near Lille and Paris and on the following night bombed various targets in France and Belgium.

By the time the Mosquitoes, Lancasters and Halifaxes of Bomber Command returned once more to Germany, bombing Aachen and Hanover on the night of 11 April, Nuremberg had long since ceased to be headline news.

As before, the nightly RAF bomber streams flowed on across the length and breadth of a reeling but still dogged Germany.

8   The Post-Mortems

Traditionally, a military near-catastrophe on the scale of the ill-fated RAF attack on Nuremberg inevitably becomes the subject of retrospective speculation, controversy, analysis, recriminations, distortion and often legend.

Such was never the case with Nuremberg.

To the best of the author's knowledge, the Nuremberg disaster—which could perhaps be regarded as an over-emphasis in terminology unless you had happened to have been a participant in the operation—has until recently only been the subject of incidental comment in publications concerning the conduct of the British strategic bombing offensive in Europe during World War II.

Some war-time British and German air war leaders were subsequently moved to make comment. One such competent opinion was frankly and forcibly expressed by Air Vice-Marshal D. C. T. Bennett, CB, CBE, DSO, in his book *Pathfinder*, published after the war by Frederick Muller Ltd, London. Although the dynamic founder and leader of the war-time Pathfinder Force did not hesitate to make perfectly clear where he thought the blame for the Nuremberg losses lay, he kept it within the perspectives of the European air war as a whole.

It would be beyond the author's competence to quote this and other expert opinions merely in the interests of provoking controversy. He is interested, however, in the reasons why the air battle for Nuremberg has for so many years merely gathered dust in the yellowed pages of old newspapers.

There could have been several reasons.

Occurring as it did at the close of Bomber Command's bitter and bloody involvement in the so-called Battle of Berlin during the first three months of 1944, losses at Nuremberg could well have seemed entirely in proportion to those suffered by the Command since the bleak dawn of the year— 763 Lancasters and Halifaxes shot down in the first twelve weeks of 1944.

As the last major attack on Germany for that winter and with Bomber Command still licking its wounds and preparing for the pre-invasion bombing campaign against transportation targets in enemy-occupied France and Belgium, the Nuremberg attack was speedily overtaken and overshadowed by the march of events towards D-Day.

In any case, taking the allied strategic bombing offensive in Europe as a whole, the RAF losses on Nuremberg were not, proportionately, as cataclysmic as those which had jolted the Americans on 14 October 1943 when 60 out of 280 of their bombers had failed to return from Schweinfurt, the last occasion on which the USAAF was to fly deep-penetration missions over Germany without fighter escort all the way.

However, the comparison is not entirely valid. The American losses were sustained as a result of pressing on despite knowledge of the RAF's hard-won experience that daylight raids deep into Germany without fighter escort were simply 'not on'.

The RAF attack on Nuremberg, on the other hand, was planned and carried out with due respect for the quality of the known German air defences and executed within the limits of Bomber Command's operational capabilities. By 30 March 1944 Bomber Command was implacably and grimly in the business of dropping bombs to knock Germany out of the war and was not guilty of launching operations that had only a marginal chance of success, with a minimal result, in the interests of reaping a harvest of headlines.

As this narrative is mainly from the perspective of the aircrews who flew and fought in the 'Nuremberg massacre', as so many of them came to call it, perhaps the last words are best heard from Marshal of the RAF, Sir Arthur Harris GCB, OBE, AFC, the man who commanded Bomber

Command on that desperate night. In a letter to the author from a whimsically appropriate address—Goring on Thames, in the lush and pastoral Oxfordshire countryside—the wartime bomber chief stated, inter alia:

'It was a perpetual source of astonishment to me during my $3\frac{1}{2}$ years as Commander-in-Chief, Bomber Command, that we did not suffer many more heavy reverses of the Nuremberg type and I cannot understand why the German defences did not improve much more rapidly and effectively as the bomber war developed over three long and terrible years.

'In Bomber Command we had to lay on and, more often than not, carry through, at least one and occasionally more than one major battle every twenty-four hours. That was a situation which no naval or military command has ever had to compete with. Navies fight two or three major battles per war. Armies, maybe a dozen. We had to lay on, during my $3\frac{1}{2}$ years, well over *a thousand*. Naturally enough, we occasionally got a badly bloodied nose—but nothing like what we gave the Boche.

'There was a limit—and a small one—to the choice of tactical changes which we could introduce from time to time and occasionally such tactical changes had therefore to include doing something which the enemy would probably think so obvious that it would be the last thing we would ever choose to do.

'In the Nuremberg show we chose wrong and the Boche, aided by unexpectedly bad weather, guessed right.

'It is a wonder that coincidence did not occur more often during the thousand and more major battles which we fought . . .'

Glossary

ACP: Aerodrome Control Point, a control van parked near the holding point of a runway in use from which aircraft were cleared visually for take-off by flashing Aldis lamp. (Bomber Command's operational take-offs were customarily carried out under conditions of strict radio silence so that the Luftwaffe radio monitors would not be alerted by a sudden and massive increase in the volume of the Command's radio traffic.)

AIRBORNE CIGAR: Airborne transmitter, carried by aircraft of special-duties squadrons of Bomber Command, which jammed Luftwaffe air-ground night-fighter radio control frequencies.

BANDITS: Enemy aircraft; in Bomber Command's case, Luftwaffe intruders which had infiltrated the returning bomber stream to attack either the bases or the home-coming bombers at their most vulnerable disadvantage—gear and flaps down, low and slow, in the circuit area.

BOOZER: Radar device fitted to RAF bombers which activated a system of flashing lights to warn pilots of the approach of enemy aircraft.

CONE: A concentration of searchlight beams on a single bomber, usually in cooperation with flak defences.

COOKIE: A 4000-pound, high-blast, light-case, British 'block-buster' bomb; sometimes referred to by the Germans as a 'mine' although it was a free-fall weapon unlike the equivalent Luftwaffe 'landmine' which was dropped by parachute over English targets.

DULAG LUFT: Durchlager Luftwaffe or air force transit camp. As Dulag Luft, Frankfurt-on-Main.

FISHPOND: Radar device fitted to RAF bombers, usually monitored by wireless air gunner of crew, which gave visual warning of the approach of enemy aircraft.

GARDENING: Bomber Command code-name for its anti-shipping, mine-laying sorties in enemy waters.

HELLE NACHTJAGD: Luftwaffe code-name for system of illuminated night-fighting.

HIMMELBETT ('Four-poster bed'): Luftwaffe code-name for tactic of ground-controlled night-fighting in 'boxes' of the Kammhuber Line.

H2S: RAF radar bombing aid which, regardless of fog, cloud or darkness, 'painted' an electronic picture of the terrain over which a bomber so equipped was flying.

KITE: RAF slang for an aircraft and successor to the 1914–18 Royal Flying Corps 'bus'; e.g. 'We had the fastest kite on the squadron'.

MONICA: Radar device fitted to Bomber Command aircraft which gave an audible and urgent 'pipping' on the crew's intercom to warn of the approach of enemy aircraft from astern.

NEWHAVEN: Ground-marking of target aiming-points with flares or target indicators dropped 'blind' using H2S, with subsequent visual confirmation.

NFT: Night Flying Test; day-time flight test by a crew of their aircraft and its equipment prior to a night flight, particularly before operations.

OBOE: British 'blind-bombing' radar aid.

OKW: Oberkommando Wehrmacht, or High Command, Armed Forces.

OTU: Operational Training Unit, usually equipped, in the case of Bomber Command, with Vickers Wellingtons.

PARRAMATTA: Ground-marking of target aiming-point by target indicators dropped 'blind' with the aid of OBOE.

PFF: Pathfinder Force.

R/T: Radio telephony for air-ground voice communications.

SCARECROWS: British code-name for German flak shells which, on time-fused explosion, simulated an exploding British bomber so as to dismay inexperienced crews.

SCHRAGE MUSIK ('Jazz Music'): German code-name for tactic of mounting fixed, nearly vertical, upward-firing cannon in fuselages of night fighters for close-range, under-belly attacks on unsuspecting RAF bombers. In the opinion of some authorities this was first used during the Nuremberg operation.

SPOOF: A feint attack by the RAF to divert German night fighters from the target actually intended.

TI: Target-indicator flare, deployed in a variety of colour combinations, used by PFF to mark aiming-points of target areas.

WANGANUI: Tactic of dropping 'sky-markers' blindly using OBOE when ground TIS would have been obscured by overcast, fog, smog, or smoke.

WILDE SAU ('Wild Boar'): Code-name for Luftwaffe night fighters originally flung into action over illuminated target areas on a freelance, free-roving, target-of-opportunity basis of visual interception.

WINDOW: British code-name for tactic of dropping strips of tin foil to swamp and confuse German radar defences.

WUERZBERG: German radar for direction of night fighters, flak and searchlights.

ZAHME SAU ('Tame Boar'): Code-name for Luftwaffe night fighters operating under radar control for interception of the bomber stream to and from the target.

Bibliography

Books and other publications consulted by the author for background information and, in some cases, quoted:

Lawrence, W. J., *No. 5 Bomber Group*, Faber & Faber, London, 1951.

Harris, Sir Arthur, GCB, OBE, AFC, Marshal of the RAF, *Bomber Offensive*, Collins, London, 1947.

Saward, Dudley, Group Captain, OBE, *The Bomber's Eye*, Cassell, London, 1959.

Irving, David, *The Destruction of Dresden*, William Kimber, 1963.

Johnson, Frank, *RAAF Over Europe*, Eyre & Spottiswoode, London, 1946.

Payne, L. G. S., Air Commodore, CBE, MC, AFC, *Air Dates*, Heinemann, London, 1957.

Herington, John, *Air War Against Germany and Italy*, Volume III, Australian War Memorial, Canberra, 1954.

Verrier, Anthony, *The Bomber Offensive*, B. T. Batsford Ltd, London, 1968.

The Aeroplane, Temple Press Ltd, issue of April 7, 1944.

Appendix: The Survivors

This appendix contains further information about those survivors of the RAF attack on Nuremberg who were kind enough to complete questionnaires from the author. Their names are listed in alphabetical order with subsequent ranks and decorations, post-war occupations and last addresses known to the author:

ALLISON, John G.: RAF. (Subsequent rank, decorations, post-war employment and last address not known to author. Narrative by courtesy of M.A. Garbett Esq., Solihull, Warwickshire, England.)

BARCLAY, William John: RAAF; Flight Lieutenant; DFC; accountant then air traffic control officer; 88 Scott Street Beaumaris, 3193, Melbourne, Victoria, Australia.

BARKER, Harold James: RAAF; DFC and bar; navigator with Qantas Airways, Australia.

BEDDIS, Howard John: RAF; Warrant Officer; assurance representative; 14 Fir Grove, King's Heath, Birmingham 14, Warwickshire, England. (Shot down over Amiens, France, on the night of 10 April 1944.)

BOWMAN, Arthur Rhodes Sydney: RAAF; Flight Lieutenant; DFC; grazier; 'Archerfield', Singleton, New South Wales, Australia.

BRILL, William Lloyd: RAAF; Group Captain; DSO, DFC and bar; regular officer, RAAF; while Officer Commanding, RAAF, Townsville, Queensland and Senior Air Staff Officer, North Queensland area, died at Canberra, ACT, on 12 October 1964.

BURROWS, Stephen: RAF. (Subsequent rank, decorations, post-war employment and last address not known to the author. Narrative by courtesy of M.A. Garbett Esq.)

CALLAWAY, Roger Bouldin: RCAF; Flying Officer; farmer; Box 1003, RCAF Station, Cold Lake, Alberta, Canada.

CHRISTNER, A. Lyle: RCAF; Flying Officer; engineer; Sault Sainte Marie, Ontario, Canada.

COLLIS, Frank: RAF; Flight Lieutenant; DFC and Mentioned in Dispatches; policeman; 48 Sherrards Way, Barnet, Hertfordshire, England.

CONWAY, Daniel Thomas: RAAF; Flight Lieutenant; DFC; civil servant; The Residency, Alice Springs, Northern Territory, Australia.

CURLING, Raymond: RAAF; Flight Lieutenant; DFC; salesman; Hazeldene via Broadford, Victoria, Australia.

DANIELS, Sidney Patrick: RAF; rank last known to author, Wing Commander; DSO and bar, DFC and bar; 7 Holmfield Avenue, Leicester, England.

DAVIDSON, David George: RAF; Warrant Officer; aircraft fitter; 10 Culduthel Road, Inverness, Scotland.

DOUBLEDAY, Arthur William: RAAF; Wing Commander; DSO, DFC; farmer and grazier until 1948, then Director, Department of Civil Aviation, Commonwealth of Australia; 4 Canberra Crescent, East Lindfield, New South Wales, Australia.

DYKES, George: RCAF; Flying Officer; department store employee; 1778 Bloor Street West, Toronto, Canada.

EARL, John Gordon: RAAF; Flying Officer; Mentioned in Dispatches; builder, then grazier and company director.

FORREST, Henry Thomas: RAF, Flight Lieutenant; DFC; radio and television dealer; 110 Higher Road, Halewood, Liverpool, England.

FORSYTH, Dudley Thomas: RAAF; Group Captain; DFC; student, then public servant; 20 Walsh Street, South Yarra, Victoria, Australia.

GIRARDAU, Denis Eyre: RAAF; Flight Lieutenant; DFC; motor school proprietor; 1 Rothesay Avenue, East Malvern, Victoria, Australia.

GOLDSMITH, John Edward: RCAF; Wing Commander; DFC, AFC; regular officer, RCAF; RCAF Station, Senneterre,

Quebec, Canada.

GUNDELACH, Carlos Patricio: RAAF; Squadron Leader; regular officer, RAAF; RAAF, Darwin, Northern Territory, Australia.

HAYES, Brian John Francis Xavier: RAAF; Wing Commander; DFM; regular officer, RAAF; Department of Air, Canberra, ACT, Australia. In Novembe 1944 Hayes was shot down over Hamburg on his 89th operational trip when flak hit and exploded a load of target indicator marker flares in his aircraft's bomb bay. He was a POW at Dulag Luft, Frankfurt-on-Main, at Stalag Luft III, Sagan, in lower Silesia and at Stalag III A, Luckenwalde, south of Berlin.

HAZELWOOD, Edgar Charles: RAF; Warrant Officer; stores clerk; Boston, Lincolnshire, England.

JENNINGS, Geoffrey: RAF; Flight Sergeant; capstan operator; 25 Cumbria Close, Maidenhead, Berkshire, England.

JOHNSON, Sydney Harley: RAAF; Flight Lieutenant; DFC and bar; solicitor; Port Moresby, Papua New Guinea.

KNIGHTS, Robin Herbert: RAF; DFC and bar, AFC; civil airline pilot and farmer; Kuching, Sarawak, Borneo.

LAMBERT, John Leonard: RAF; Flight Lieutenant; chartered accountant; 14 Boundary Gardens, Newcastle-upon-Tyne, England. Shot down during the Nuremberg operation, Lambert was a prisoner at Dulag Luft, Frankfort-on-Main, Stalag Luft VI E and VI A and Stalag 357.

LIPMAN, Sidney: RAF; Warrant Officer; builder; 35 Heathland Road, London, England.

McHATTIE, Robert: RAF; Flying Officer: DFC; police constable; Rosehall Farm, Keith, Banffshire, Scotland.

MACKINNON, Harry Bertram: RAF; Squadron Leader; DFC; cost accountant; 125 Gillott Road, Edgbaston, Birmingham 16, England.

McLAUCHLAN, John Gilchrist: RCAF; Flying Officer; telephone traffic supervisor; 354 14th Street, Brandon, Manitoba, Canada. Shot down on the Nuremberg operation, McLauchlan was interrogated at Dulag Luft, Frankfurt-on-Main, and subsequently a prisoner at Stalag Luft VI, Heydekrug and Stalag 357, surviving a lengthy march across Germany, towards the war's end.

MACLEAN, James Stuart: RAF; Warrant Officer; representative; The Wishing Well, Woolaby, Brigg, Lincolnshire, England.

MAXWELL, J.H.: RCAF; Flight Lieutenant, fighter controller, Semi Automatic Ground Environment, RCAF HQ, North Bay, Ontario, Canada; 818 Ski Club Road, North Bay.

MOORHOUSE, Samuel Arthur: RAAF; acting Flight Lieutenant, substantive Flying Officer; DFC; finance company director; 8 Don Court, Caulfield, Victoria, Australia.

MORREY, Eric: RAF; Warrant Officer; transport manager; 8 Ryebank Avenue, Crewe, Cheshire, England.

MORRISBY, Walter Frank: RAAF; Flying Officer; Mentioned in Dispatches; clerk; 9 Ormond Street, Bellerive, Tasmania, Australia.

MUSTARD, Ernest Andrew: RAAF; Flight Lieutenant; DFC; cost clerk; 12 Parker Street, Ormond, Victoria, Australia.

OGILVIE, William Donald: RAF; Warrant Officer. After being shot down on the Nuremberg raid, Warrant Officer Ogilvie was captured, interrogated at Dulag Luft, Frankfurt-on-Main and imprisoned in a number of camps including Stalag III A, Luckenwalde, south of Berlin, and survived a long march across Germany in the last bitter winter of the war.

PARISSIEN, Reginald Walter: RAF; Warrant Officer; civil servant; 2 Bassett Way, Slough, Buckinghamshire, England. He was shot down subsequent to the Nuremberg raid.

PLOWRIGHT, Philip Edward: RAF; Flight Lieutenant; DFC; Horticulturist and Supervisor of Grounds, University of Birmingham, Warwickshire, England.

PRATT, Leonard Albert: RAF; Flying Officer; assistant plant manager; 'Pedwar', Ash Road, Hartley, near Dartford, Kent, England.

PRICE, Reginald William Douglas; RCAF; Pilot Officer; DFC; regular officer, RAF, until 1951, then RCAF; 28 Glen Road, Belleville, Ontario Canada.

RICHARDSON, Donald Samuel: RAF; Squadron Leader; DFC; audit clerk; 1 Winchester Close, Amesbury, Salisbury, Wiltshire, England.

RUDD, Ronald Beattie: RCAF; Flight Lieutenant; civilian instructor, RCAF; 29 Whitehead Street, Clinton, Ontario, Canada. Subsequent to the Nuremberg raid, Rudd was shot down and taken prisoner in May 1944.

SHAW, Frederick: RCAF; Flight Sergeant; civil servant; 147 Don Street, North Kamloops, British Columbia, Canada.

STENNING, William Albert: RAF; Flying Officer; automotive sales manager; Kessingland, Hascombe, Godalming, Surrey, England.

STUART, Fredrick Robert: RAAF; acting Squadron Leader, substantive Flight Lieutenant; regular officer, RAAF; No. 23 (Auxiliary) Squadron, RAAF, Amberley, Queensland, Australia. Subsequent to the Nuremberg raid, Stuart was shot down on 24 May, 1944, and taken prisoner. After interrogation at Dulag Luft, Frankfurt-on-Main, where he spent a month in solitary confinement for being 'an insolent and decadent swine', he spent the rest of the war as a prisoner-of-war in camps including Stalag VI J at Gerresheim, near Dusseldorf.

STRICKLAND, Alan Geoffrey: RAAF; DFC and American DFC; public servant; 4 Princess Avenue, Highett, Victoria, Australia.

WEBB, Harry: RAF; Flight Lieutenant; HQ Air Forces, Borneo; BFPO 660.

WESLEY, Joseph: RAF; Flying Officer; DFC; engineering assistant; 6 Walnut Green, Pine Ridge, Bushey, Hertfordshire, England.

WHITLOCK, Sidney Nicholas: RAF; Warrant Officer; transport supervisory clerk; 48 The Willoughbys, Upper Richmond Road West; East Sheen, London SW 14, England. After being shot down on the Nuremberg raid, Warrant Officer Whitlock was interrogated at Dulag Luft, Frankfurt-on-Main, and later imprisoned at Stalag Luft VI, Heydekrug, in Lithuania, Stalag 357, Thorn, in Poland and at Fallingbostel, north of Hannover, Germany.

WRIGHT, Reuben William: RCAF; Wing Commander; DFC, DFM, CD; regular officer, RCAF; Box 1648, RCAF Station, North Bay, Ontario, Canada.

ZAMIATIN, Victor Vladimir: RAAF; Warrant Officer; clerk, Department of Civil Aviation, Commonwealth of Australia.